Sindh Bani

Sarla Kripalani was born in Karachi in 1930, a gentlewoman of Sindh and a lifelong custodian of its culture and memory. Educated at a convent school under the care of Irish nuns, she grew up in a world that was soon to be irrevocably changed. In 1946, on the cusp of the Partition of India, Sarla was sent to Indore to live in safety with her grandmother. There, she completed her Bachelor of Arts and married in 1952, returning to a Pakistan newly severed from India.

In December 1963, Sarla and her family escaped from Pakistan and settled in Mumbai. She was the beloved wife of a doctor, a devoted mother and the gracious matriarch who bound her extended family together with warmth and wisdom.

Sarla's hands were never idle. She brought her innate creativity to life through painting, embroidery, cooking and, above all, writing. Throughout her life, she remembered Sindh—the land, its stories and its spirit—and recorded her recollections with tenderness and insight.

A storehouse of memory and tradition, Sarla Kripalani remains a voice of love, longing and luminous storytelling from a land that was once her own.

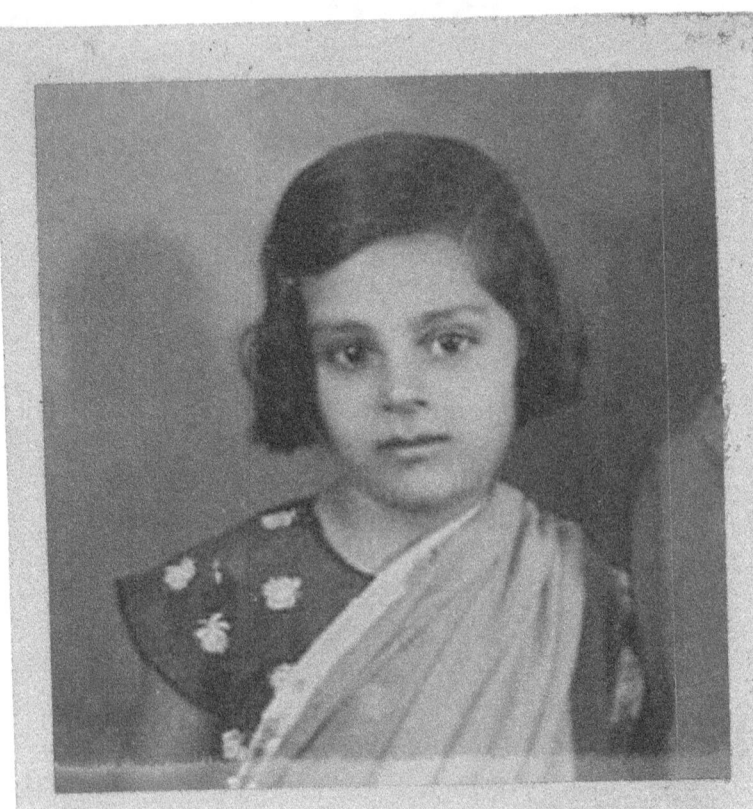

A young Sarla

Sindh Bani
AN ANTHOLOGY

SARLA KRIPALANI

Published by
Rupa Publications India Pvt. Ltd 2025
161-B/4, Gulmohar House,
Yusuf Sarai Community Centre,
New Delhi 110049

Sales centres:
Bengaluru Chennai
Hyderabad Kolkata Mumbai

Edition copyright © Manjeet Kripalani 2025

Originally written in Sindhi by T.K. Mirchandani, *Sindhwork and Sindhworkis* was published in 1920, and translated by Sarla Kripalani in 2001. Sindhi original © Literary estate of T.K. Mirchandani. English translation copyright © Manjeet Kripalani.

Photographs courtesy: Manjeet Kripalani

Copyright of the photographs vests with the respective photographer/copyright owner. While every effort has been made to trace copyright holders and obtain permission, this has not been possible in all cases; any omissions brought to our attention will be remedied in future editions.

The views and opinions expressed in this book are the author's own and the facts are as reported by her, which have been verified to the extent possible, and the publishers are not in any way liable for the same.

All rights reserved.
No part of this publication may be reproduced, transmitted or stored in a retrieval system, in any form or by any means, electronic, mechanical, photocopying, recording or otherwise, without the prior permission of the publisher.

P-ISBN: 978-93-7003-639-0
E-ISBN: 978-93-7003-103-6

First impression 2025

10 9 8 7 6 5 4 3 2 1

Printed in India

This book is sold subject to the condition that it shall not, by way of trade or otherwise, be lent, resold, hired out or otherwise circulated, without the publisher's prior consent, in any form of binding or cover other than that in which it is published.

Contents

Foreword 9

Short Stories of Sindh

1. The Many Capitals of Sindh 17
2. Karachee, Glory of the East 19
3. Quetta, Picnics and Pathans 22
4. Kunwar Bhagat 25
5. Pir Pagaro 29
6. Amil Zamindars 31
7. Preparing for Partition, Karachi to Indore 33
8. Dewan Mulchand 38
9. Dewan Doulatram and The Big House 40
10. The Joint Family 44
11. Peel Pawas 46
12. The Neem Tree 49
13. The Anglo-Indians 51
14. Bombay Delights 53
15. Mirs and Dr Manghanmal 56
16. The Journey of No Return 59
17. The Hooris of Sindh 62
18. Transvestites 65
19. Hyderabad, Banaras and Dr Nari 68
20. Dewan Gobindram and Narayan 71
21. Prabha 76
22. Vijay Kapoor 79
23. Nimoo Sadarangani 83
24. Ratna Mukhi 86
25. Kala 88

Aaya Pir, Bhagga Mir and Other Sindhi Proverbs

Foreword 94
Preface 95
Introduction 97
Sindhi Proverbs and Their English Equivalents 101
Sindhi Proverbs That Are Culturally Unique and Have No English Equivalent 190

Sindhwork and Sindhworkis

Foreword 200
Author's Note 202
1. How Did the Word 'Sindhworki' Originate? 204
2. The Spread of Sindhworkis 205
3. The Advantage of Sindhwork 206
4. The Moving Salesman 207
5. Advantages of Pherie 208
6. Taking Advantage of Sindhworki Partners 210
7. The Advantage of Sindhworki Illiteracy 211
8. Reasons Why Sindhworki Children Were Illiterate ... 212
9. Reasons for Illiteracy of Sethia Children 213
10. For Correspondence and Bookkeeping, the Clerical Staff Must Be Bhaiband and Not Amil 214
11. The Jealousies among Sindhworkis 216
12. Alcoholism among Sindhworkis 218
13. The Outcome of Alcoholism 219
14. Wealth at All costs 220
15. Reasons for the Lack of Savings 221
16. The True Story of a Salesman: An Autobiography ... 223
17. Sethias Deliberately Ruined the Pheriewallah System ... 229
18. State of Sindhworki 'Servants' 237
19. To Take Work Against Business Norms Does Not Bring About Much Profit 240

20.	Who Is a Sindhworki Thief?	242
21.	The Behaviour of Servants	243
22.	Why Do They Employ Local Staff?	245
23.	Lack of Proper Accounts Gives the Servants an Opportunity to Slacken, and Then to Vice	246
24.	Sindhworki Partners	248
25.	Agreements/Contracts for Partnership	250
26.	Partner Gains 40 Per Cent (6 Annas out of a Rupee) but Pays 50 Per Cent (8 Annas out of a Rupee) by Way of Loss	252
27.	Partnership Agreements Are Redundant	254
28.	Injustices Against the Sindhworkis	255
29.	A Critical Analysis	266
30.	The Outcome	267
31.	Lack of Education Is the Cause of the Faulty System	268
32.	Sindhworkis Are Traitors	270
33.	'Desh Hateshta' or 'Uncaring of Your Own': What Kind of Bird Is That?	272
34.	Lack of Humanity in Sindhwork Sethias	275
35.	Inherent Drawbacks of Sindhworkis	278
36.	Comparison Between the Sethias of Yore and the Sethias of Today	279
37.	Soul-Searching	282
38.	Family Life of Sindhworkis	283
39.	Religious Zeal in Sindhworkis	285
40.	Sindhwork Merchants Association	286
41.	Penance	293

Acknowledgements 295
Glossary 296

Foreword

Sarla Kripalani had a prodigious memory. She remembered experiences and places from when she was one year old. She remembered her life in Sindh, where she grew up as a girl in dresses and hats, studying in a convent school. She remembered the starched damask table covers at her grandfather's official dinner parties, and the meals that were served. She remembered her departure from Sindh to Indore at the age of fifteen, when the Partition of India became inevitable. She remembered returning to Sindh as a young bride of twenty-one, arms and legs covered this time, as a result of a new societal structure. She remembered the 52 letters of the Sindhi alphabet, written in the Arabic script, which gave the language such vibrancy, nuance and exactitude of expression.

Sarla absorbed the hundreds of proverbs spoken every day by the family elders, most specifically her mother, Guli, and her mother-in-law, Sarsati. She remembered the diverse communities of Sindh—the music, the food, the embroideries, the arts, the desert air, the *feel* of Sindh. She remembered all the joys and sorrows of her homeland, which she was eventually forced to leave.

Over the years in her new home in Bombay (now Mumbai), Sarla preserved these memories. Then she began to collect them in various forms. The Sindhworki translation was her first work, based on the experiences of the author, Tekchand Karamchand Mirchandani, about a system they both knew only too well. She collected proverbs over a span of 17 years, consulting family and community elders to verify their exact meanings. She found their English equivalents, uncovering in the process a profound truth: that all proverbs are universal. She placed the equivalents beside the original Sindhi proverbs, adding Hindi scripts so that future

With my mother, the author of this book

generations of assimilated Sindhis spread all over the world might know their culture and their language.

In the family, the collection of proverbs was identified as 'Sarla's obsession', an opportunity to tease her. 'Oh is this sentence also a proverb for Sarla? But it has no equivalent in English!' So, into the dustbin it went. But there were so many keepers, and these were instead included in a book printed exclusively for her. She subsequently gathered all the stalwarts of the Sindhi community at the Royal Bombay Yacht Club on a rainy day in August 2011. They relived the glory of their language and were delighted by the nearly-lost recollections. Many remembered the more precise proverbs.

The book of short stories narrates tales from the family—all the ones that we grew up hearing about the Kripalani, Bhavnani and Vaswani clans. She hand-wrote them on recycled paper, on the backs of bills, on scraps of paper as soon as she remembered something. She also wrote the stories of other Sindhis, especially when they were connected to her own. It was a labour of love, of longing, written without rancour—just the facts, and recollections that delighted or impressed.

The Sindhi Hindu community has shrunk. We have no homeland of our own, no state patronage, and very few to love the language and culture that existed for hundreds of years in that blessed land. The Pakistani state has neglected to preserve the land of Mohenjo-daro—Sindhi for Mound of the Dead—that ancient civilization that emerged from the fertile Indus Valley.

This anthology, a collection of three books, is published posthumously. It is a homage to my mother, Sarla Kripalani, and my father and her beloved partner, Dr Nari M. Kripalani, who ensured we grew up knowing our heritage, no matter how distant it had become, and no matter how assimilated we had become in our new motherland. This is a gift, as Sarla intended, for current and future generations of Sindhis everywhere: that they may always remember that the spirit residing in our souls is centuries old, has survived before, will continue to survive and, through their love and interest, flourish once again.

—**Manjeet Kripalani**
Co-Founder, Gateway House:
Indian Council on Global Relations;
Former India Bureau Chief, *BusinessWeek*

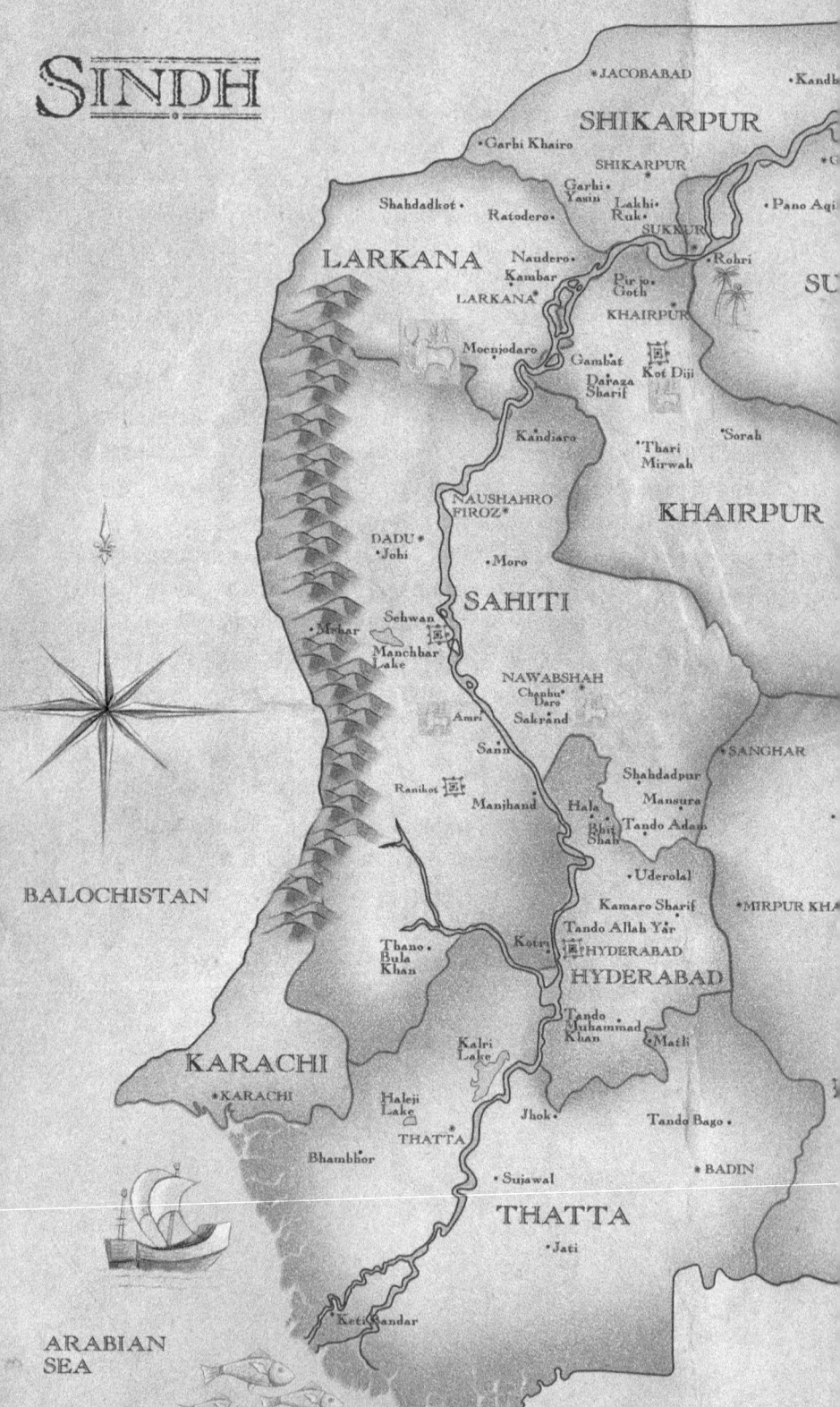

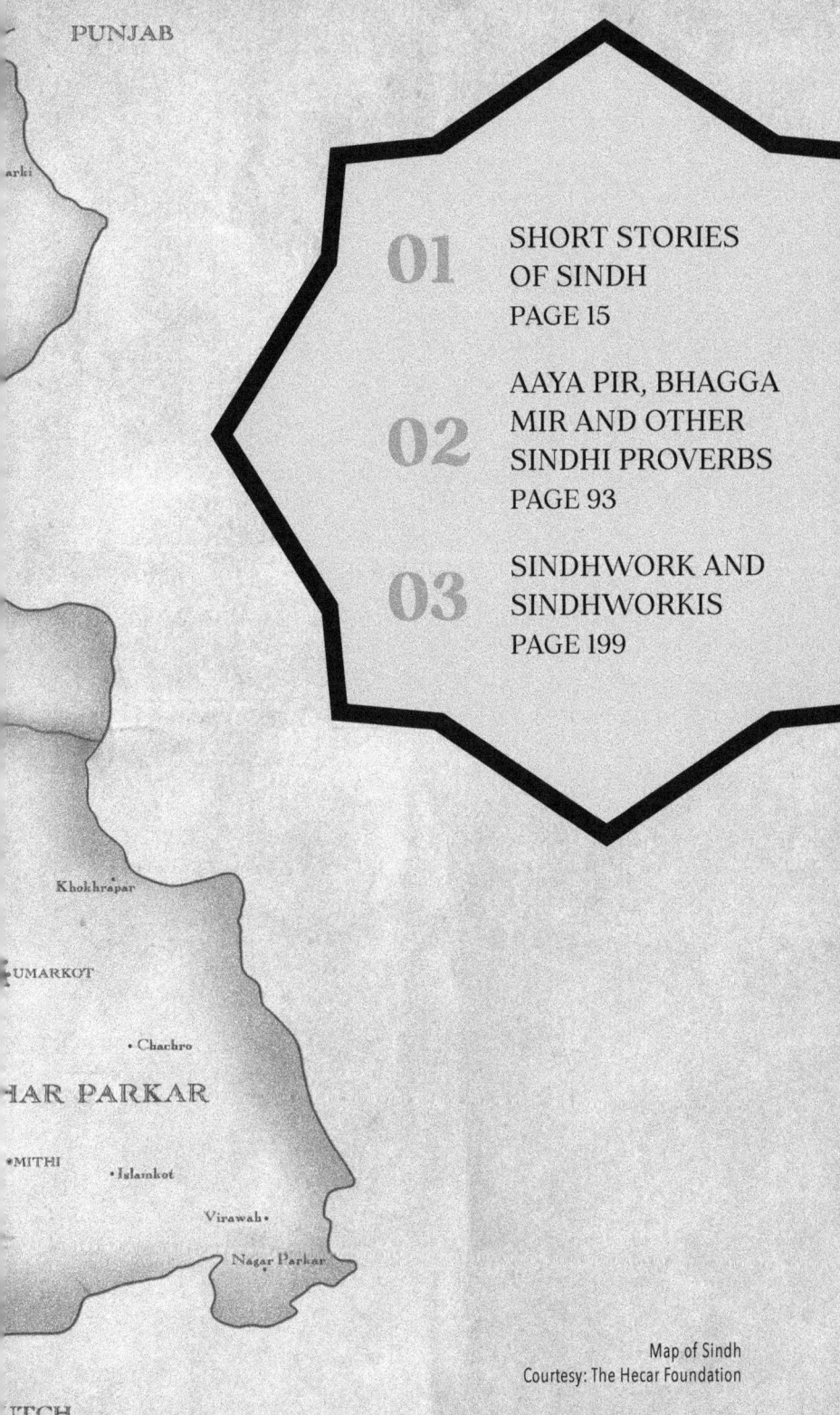

01	SHORT STORIES OF SINDH PAGE 15
02	AAYA PIR, BHAGGA MIR AND OTHER SINDHI PROVERBS PAGE 93
03	SINDHWORK AND SINDHWORKIS PAGE 199

Map of Sindh
Courtesy: The Hecar Foundation

Sarla, newly-married, 1952

Short stories of Sindh

Sarla Kripalani

An artist's representation of the Pukka Fort, built on top of a hillock around which the city of Hyderabad, Sindh (now in Pakistan), came up. The fort was built in 1768 using pukka, or burnt, bricks, which gave it its name–Pakko Qilo in Sindhi and Pakka Qila in Urdu. It was famed for its large halls and palaces, majestic ramparts and beautiful murals.

The Many Capitals of Sindh

In AD 1759, the capital of Sindh was the town of Thatta. The then Muslim ruling party set the city on fire by tying rags to sparrows' legs. It was to show the local Hindu populace to comply with their wishes as they were all-powerful.

A new capital, Khudabad, was established on the east bank of the mighty Indus, near the town of Hala. Hala was famous for its lathe and lacquer-work furniture.

Every Sindhi household had a lacquer-work *pingha*, a six-foot cradle suspended on a stand, large enough to allow an adult to sleep on it comfortably. As there was no dearth of domestic help, a fancy cord would be tied to the edge of the *pingha* and a domestic worker would gently rock it while the adult took forty winks. Even the poorest of the poor would invest in one such piece, if only to serve as a conversation starter.

Unfortunately, Khudabad was submerged in 1789 by the changing course of the Indus river. The new ruler of Sindh, Mir Fateh Ali Khan Talpur, then moved the capital to Hyderabad (formerly Nerankot). Hyderabad has withstood the vagaries of time and stands to this day as a monument to Sindh. It is now a part of Pakistan.

Hyderabad was to Sindh what Paris is to France—the hub of fashion. It was often spoken of as *nar, naar, narai* and *phul*.

> **Nar:** the men of *nagar* who were well boned, handsome and valiant.
> **Naar:** the women as beautiful as those of the town of Nasarpur.
> **Narai:** the women whose eyes were as well shaped and sparkling as those of women of the Narai tribe.
> **Phul:** fruits as juicy as those grown in Fateh Baug.

Nasarpur, a town near Hala, was well known for its hand-woven, cotton and silk *khes*, a top covering used in the harsh summer months. It was of multicoloured hues, non-bleeding and reversible. A work of art. It had no 'right' or 'wrong' side, just the symmetry of pattern.

A unique architectural feature of Hyderabad was the *mungh*. These were terrace constructions—usually on the ground or first floors—enclosed on the north and east sides but open to the south and west, allowing the cool south-westerly winds to funnel down to the rooms below. This acted as a natural air-conditioning system and became a hallmark of Hyderabad. As one approached the outskirts of the city—by car or train—the sight of the munghs signalled that home was near.

At the Battle of Miani, Sir Charles Napier defeated the Talpurs, marking the beginning of British rule in Sindh, which lasted till 1947, when the British left the country in turmoil.

Karachee, Glory of the East

In 1843, the then Governor of Sindh Sir Charles Napier wrote, 'Karachee, thou shalt be the glory of the East! Would that I could come again to see your grandeur!'

Karachi (earlier *Karachee*, a shortened and corrupted version of the original name *Kolachi-jo-Goth*), up to 1947—the time of Partition—was a lovely, clean city of gardens and beaches. An old-fashioned lighthouse in Manora, across the creek from Kiamari, was a popular picnic spot and boats would ferry picnickers there for the day. Karachi then had a population of less than a million. Now, it is bursting at the seams with over seven million inhabitants, maybe more.

After Partition, the capital of Sindh shifted from Hyderabad to Karachi. The seat of government subsequently moved to Islamabad, which was perhaps strategically better. Thus, Karachi—with its natural harbour where ocean liners could dock and avail of the facility of a dry dock—became the financial capital of Pakistan, comparable to Bombay.

When the British took over Sindh, because of its strategic position, Karachi became a military station, with hostels and barracks established in the old city on Burns Road. I believe it was earlier known as Band Road due to soldiers marching with a band. Later, it came to be called Banned Road, apparently because the area housed nautch girls and was declared off-limits to soldiers!

A camp was set up in the modern city of Karachi, far from Banned Road and its temptations, and the troops were moved to a more secure area. The road was renamed after some deserving officer as Burns Road. The call girls were relocated, the road widened and beautiful gardens set up. One such vineyard and garden was the famed Burns Garden. The grapes from this garden were famous for their colour, a deep burgundy, and taste—oh so juicy and sweet—and the fragrance surpassed that of any rose *attar*. It was said that the fertilizer used contained real goat's blood.

The camp area was a delight. It had a shopping centre called Saddar Bazaar, where one could buy anything—from a needle to an elephant! Beyond this was Frere Hall and Library Gardens, which was frequented by the gentry. The ladies would take a turn while the children, under the supervision of their *ayahs*, played on the well-manicured lawns. At sundown, the ladies would join their husbands at the club next door. It was later converted

Frere Road in 1902. It leads to Clifton which (as can be seen on the horizon) was largely barren. In the 1930s, Clifton Bridge was built to connect the city centre with Clifton.

into Hope Lodge—a Freemasons' Hall, or as the locals called it, *bhoot khana*. A modern clubhouse was built down the road, with facilities for tennis and badminton, and was named the Karachi Club, which still exists.

Further on from Frere Hall was Clifton Bridge. It was actually an overbridge spanning the railway tracks, at the end of which was Clifton Crossing.

Clifton Crossing was a vast open ground, closed to vehicular traffic. Cars would park at the edge of the ground. Children learnt to ride bicycles there, teenagers practised driving, and elders took evening walks in the cool sea breeze.

Ahead of the crossing, the road forked. The left led to Old Clifton, home to beautiful colonial houses overlooking the sea, which stood on an elevated rocky ground.

The road on the right led to New Clifton, with modern villas and its landmark, the Mohatta Palace. A straight road from there brought one to the well-paved ground and the dome of New Clifton. From here it was walk, walk and only walk, along a wide promenade and down the steps to the beach. It was a continental shelf, making it very safe for swimmers. The water was always so clear and blue. Children would collect seashells that had washed ashore with the tide, as also the bluebottles or starfish whose sting, though not lethal, was extremely painful.

New Clifton was a popular picnic spot, especially on moonlit nights. People would form groups, take their hampers, and spend the best part of the night there.

03 Quetta, Picnics and Pathans

I was one-year-old when the family took a holiday to a town in the North-West Frontier Province, now in Pakistan. We were joined by my mother's family and some friends, and it turned out to be quite a large group. I have a faint recollection of the place we stayed—a wooden staircase with a gleaming banister leading up to a first-floor apartment, into a hall with a highly polished flooring.

The second flash is of a moonlit night—a vast ground with a backdrop of mountains, lots of people and many cars. Forty-five years later, I happened to have a conversation with my mother and mentioned the above 'flashes' from the depths of my memory. She was amazed at how a child of just one year could remember even that much! She then related what follows.

My first birthday was celebrated in Quetta. In those days, moonlit picnics were very popular. The whole paraphernalia

Picnic menu

Utensils, food, *khansamas* and bearers all travelled in a separate truck behind the family car, with all the picnic necessities. To eat during the journey were a variety of *lolis*.

1. Masala-ka-loli, eaten first as it had onions, tomatoes and coriander.
2. Namak-mirchi-ki-loli, made with salt and pepper.
3. Pheeka loli, made plain, to be eaten with honey.
4. Mithee loli, made with sugar or jaggery.

Loli: An Indian flatbread, made with *andaaz*

Three handfuls of atta, with four or five tablespoons of ghee. Knead lightly; add other ingredients—or not.

Knead until firm. Roll out with a rolling pin to ½ inch thickness. Score diagonal checks with the point of a knife, and prick with a fork to allow for even cooking.

Cook on a *tava* over a low flame, flipping only four times.

Train travel treats

On the train from Hyderabad to Karachi was Jhimpir station, famous for its *titar*. The train stopped for 20 minutes, allowing travellers to buy a food tray with roasted titar cooked in dry masalas.

The accompaniments were rice, dal, bhaji. Because it was the British Raj, the meal was served in proper plates. At the next station, Jungshahi Junction, the trays and plates would be collected, and payment would be taken for the food.

of pots and pans, crockery and cutlery would be bundled into horse-drawn buggies and cars, and transported to the chosen site. Durries would be spread out, the elders would gossip about mundane topics, and the young ones would play games, happy that—for once—the '8.00 p.m. lights out' routine did not have to be followed.

Oh! The pleasure of that feeling was indescribable.

In the meantime, the meat would be roasting and the delicacies simmering. All of a sudden, the party was surrounded by a group of Pathans—the local inhabitants. My father was a zamindar in Jacobabad, whose employees—the *haaris* or the land labourers—were mainly Muslims from the Hur tribe, once the dacoits of Sindh, but now his faithful and excellent bodyguards.

Bhavnani family picnic

My maternal grandfather was the inspector general of police. My paternal grandfather was a District and Sessions Judge and his hand-picked guards and protectors were also present. They told the Pathans to leave as this was a private party. The Pathans replied in unison, '*Mulk bhi hamara aur jaayein bhi hum?*' Translated, it literally means—'This is our land and we should be the ones to leave?'

My father had an uncanny sixth sense for danger and immediately asked everyone to pack up and strike camp. Disappointment was writ large on the faces of family and friends. They argued, what could a few Pathans do when we had an armed protection force of our own? But Daddy was adamant. With women and children around, he did not want to take any chances. We came home and had the party on our own lawns.

That ended the conversation with Mummy.

My thoughts went back in time, to my schooldays. The history of the Anglo–Afghan wars, and later, the Soviet–Afghan war, and I realized how very right Daddy had been. The ferocious nature of the tribes, the terrain of the country and the lack of knowledge Westerners had of those mountain ranges had always put them at a great disadvantage.

Osama bin Laden made a home in Afghanistan, and even with specialized weapons, a nation like the United States of America has not been successful in flushing out Al Qaeda. The Afghani terrain is known only to the local 'mountain rats'.

04 Kunwar Bhagat

Kunwar was born into a humble household at the turn of the 19th century. When he was about 10 years old, his father passed away and the responsibility of looking after his mother fell upon his young shoulders.

To earn a living, his mother would rise early in the morning and cook 2 *annas'* worth of *kohira* and before going to school he would set out to sell the lot. '*Sukhi shahookar khaeendo, duniyadar khaeendo, Rama naama ja kohira,*' with this song on his lips, he would go up and down the streets of the little town, 'the happy and rich will buy, the worldly man will buy, these peas of Lord Rama.' For every 2 annas' worth of kohira sold, he would make a profit of 4 annas. This he would give to his mother for the next day's batch and the profit was stashed away.

Recipe for Kunwar's kohira made by his mother

- Kabuli *chana* were boiled until soft, then dried.
- Coriander powder, a dusting of red chilli powder, cumin powder, and black pepper powder were added.
- The mixture was then dried again over the fire.
- She would make 2 annas' worth, and Kunwar would sell it for 4 annas.

One day, while selling the kohira, he came upon a group of learned men who were involved in a religious discourse. Kunwar sat through it and forgot all about the job at hand or even going to school. On reaching home his mother asked him for the money. He had no answer, and no memory of what had transpired.

The next day, his mother made another batch of kohira, warning him to be sure to sell it. Instead of selling it and going to school, he went to the *satsang* and listened to Sant Satramdas's discourse.

The *sant* then told him to distribute the kohira among the congregation as *prasad*. The young Kunwar did so without question. The sant was so pleased with him that he gave him one rupee—a princely sum in those days.

The lad declined, saying, 'I cannot accept monetary remuneration from my guru.' Satramdas made him understand that this was his mother's business and her livelihood and in return Kunwar could give him *guru dakshina* in the form of a promise: 'Whatever you get at this satsang henceforth, you must not take it home but leave it behind.'

Kunwar promised to do so, little realizing that this was easier said than done! One day, a lady came to the satsang and was so taken by the little boy that she made him a cap of brocade. Kunwar wore it and forgot all about it and went on his merry way. The next day, just as he was about to enter the congregation hall, Sant Satramdas stopped him, saying, 'You did not abide by your promise so you cannot enter.' The little boy was aghast.

He was told that as he had not left behind his cap, he did not qualify for entry. The young Kunwar fell at his master's feet and begged for forgiveness.

After the death of Sant Satramdas, Kunwar was honoured with the *gaddi* and became the head of the *muth*.

At that time, a Muslim saint called Pir Bhurchandi vied with Kunwar for a larger following of disciples. However, Kunwar had the charisma to attract the wild beasts, so to say. People of all castes and creeds came to him.

As is the custom of holy men, they go from place to place, preaching the name of the Lord. The roaming mendicant/minstrel Kunwar was on his way to Larkana from Shikarpur. At a station called Ruk, Pir Bhurchandi's disciples boarded the train, pretending to seek the saint's blessing. But just as the train started to move, they shot Kunwar and jumped off.

Since then Kunwar has been referred to as Shaheed Bhagat Kunwar. It is surprising that holy men could be so envious as to resort to murder.

This happened in the year 1942. Ten years later, I got married and went to live in Hyderabad in Sindh, by then a part of Pakistan. I remember another singing mendicant known as Bhagat Kunwar. In all probability, he was Pessuram Kunwar Bhagat, possibly Kunwar's son, though there is no known history of Kunwar ever having married.

Note: The Pir of Bhurchandi from Ubauro taluka in Sukkur (now Ghotki) district had a large following. He urged his *mureeds* to terrorize in the name of Islam and Allah. At that time, another *pir*—Pir Qazi Fazalullah, also of Larkana district—followed suit and asked his disciples to take up the sword in one hand and the Holy Quran in the other, with the goal of converting all 'non-believers'.

That is how the proverb *Huththa mein chhuri, kutchha mein Quran*, a knife in one hand and the Quran up one's sleeve, originated.

Tahilram Vaswani

05 Pir Pagaro

Medal awarded to Tahilram Vaswani on 3 June 1931 for capturing Pir Pagaro

Pir Pagaro was the leader of the Hur tribe of Sindh. This must have been in the early 1930s, as Tahilram Vaswani, the insepctor general of police who arrested Pir Pagaro, passed away in 1941.

Tahilram Vaswani was fair of face, extremely good-looking, with steel-grey eyes that could mesmerize. He was dashing and fearless, and earned himself the alias Gora Sahib, meaning 'the fair one', thus equating him with his British superiors.

Tahilram was asked by the then British governor of Sindh to arrest Pir Pagaro, as the Hurs had created a reign of terror in Sindh. It was like a scene from a Bollywood movie. The Hurs would come on horseback, attack and loot villages, and then vanish into their hideouts.

Tahilram found out that the Pir was hiding in a place called Sinjhoro, not too far from Hyderabad.

He took a force of his best officers and surrounded the town of Sinjhoro. He asked his men for cover, saying, 'I am going into the cave-like entrance of the hideout.' His men begged him to desist and one and all volunteered to go in his stead. But Tahilram was a noble man and would have none of it.

Short Stories of Sindh • 29

'You are as precious to your families as I am to mine, and I will not jeopardize the lives of any of my men.' So saying, he stepped into the doorway.

There was an eerie silence. In his commanding voice, Tahilram called out: 'Pir Sahib, give yourself up. I have orders to arrest you, and I will do so under any circumstance.' He heard the clicks of rifle locks of the several personal guards of the Pir who would have decimated him in a moment, but Tahilram kept walking in.

The Pir was deeply impressed. He ordered his men to lay down their arms. 'For if a person has so much courage to enter my domain alone, he must be really brave and worthy of salutation.'

Then the Pir, in his authoritative tone, called out: 'Gora Sahib, enter. I would much rather surrender to a formidable foe than kill him—which I could have easily done.' The Pir knew his time was up, and that he could not possibly be on the run all his life.

He was tried and found guilty of multiple counts of murder. Pesi Moos, ICS, exercising magisterial powers, sentenced 'The Pir of Pagaro to be hanged till death.' Pir Pagaro was hanged in Hyderabad's Central Jail under tight security. Even though the Pir had asked his people to create no trouble, a huge crowd had collected outside the jail and it was feared that the Hurs would agitate. Thus ended the reign of terror in Sindh.

06　Amil Zamindars

Most Sindhi Hindus, especially those from the Amil community, were zamindars. Theirs was usually ancestral property, handed down from father to son.

Hindus were instilled with the belief that the roof over their heads must be their own. Most of them lived in beautiful bungalows with a ground floor, first floor and a terrace room or *mungh* to catch the westerly breeze during the heat of Sindh. However, it was agricultural land that sustained this stylish way of life. Even though a pensionable job was much sought after and the educated Amil chose government service, agricultural land remained his true strength.

One such zamindar of standing was Dewan Gobindram Dialmal. His lands were in the north of Sindh—in Jacobabad, to be exact—which is now the site of a modern American airfield. His property stretched as far as the eye could see and beyond. It was prime land, perennially watered by the irrigation canals of the Sukkur barrage. He even had his own station, a railroad stop on his land called Garri Dialmal, named after his father. The train from Hyderabad to Shikarpur used to halt there for just a minute! It was a privilege reserved exclusively for the zamindar and his family.

His land shared a border with the property of Pir Pagaro, leader of the Hur tribe of Sindh. After the Pir was hanged, his tribe disbanded and sought employment. Who better to work for than the Hindu zamindars? They were considered just, paid fair wages and treated their farmhands well.

The Hurs were a hardy tribe, capable of withstanding the

harsh winters and hot summers of northern Sindh. They could work long hours under such conditions. Most of Gobindram's haaris, the labourers who tilled the land, were from the Hur tribe. They were ferocious-looking but hard-working. Like Alsatian dogs, they were known to be one-man loyalists. If they were loyal, they were very, *very* loyal, if not, they would tear you apart.

Gobindram's personal guard was a Hur. One night, as the Dewan lay in deep slumber, he sensed that all was not well. On opening his eyes, he found his bodyguard standing near his bed with the muzzle of the rifle pointed at his temple. In a calm and composed tone, the Dewan asked him, 'Maulabux, what do you want?' He did not raise his voice, nor did he jump out of bed. Maulabux replied, 'Dewan Sahib, I have a gun at your head and only have to pull the trigger, yet you ask what I desire?'

Dewan Sahib answered: 'My life is not yours to take. If God had willed it so, you would have shot me while I lay asleep. The very fact that I made you my bodyguard, gave you a loaded rifle, should have told you how much faith I repose in you. I must have found some commendable qualities in you to have done so. Now I ask you again, Maulabux, what ails you?'

Maulabux fell at Dewan Sahib's feet and asked for forgiveness, saying, 'I have yet to meet a person of such valour!'

Thenceforth, the Hur remained loyal to a fault—faithful to his master even though the Partition of 1947 brought with it deep divisions between Hindus and Muslims.

07 Preparing for Partition, Karachi to Indore

Dewan Dialmal Doulatram had predicted the Partition of India in the year 1934. He saw the unrest amongst the Muslims. He perceived that the British were losing their hold on India. Mahatma Gandhi had started the non-violence movement from Africa and the subsequent Quit India movement here in the land of his birth. Sensing the tide of change, Dialmal resigned from his job as District and Sessions Judge and decided to contest for a seat in the Sindh assembly, with the objective of giving a voice to the Hindus.

He won the election and became the agriculture minister of Sindh in 1938. This required him to move his household to Karachi, the seat of government.

After having lived in a haveli, the ministerial bungalow, though very spacious, could not compare with his home in Hyderabad. The only redeeming feature was a vast lawn bordered by flower beds, blooming with a variety of flowers. This meant there were always fresh flowers in vases all over the house—much to the pride of my mother, Dialmal's daughter-in-law.

My mother, Guli, became the official hostess as she was lettered, while my grandmother, Haribai, who had hardly been to school as she had married at the age of 10, ruled the roost. Nevertheless, Haribai's word was law and nothing escaped her.

Dewan Dialmal Doulatram

Guli was house-proud, meticulous, and a punctilious hostess.

Many were the parties held in the dining hall. Every time there would be a different setting for the sit-down dinners. Tables glistening with white damask linen, decorated sometimes with flower petals, sometimes with coloured grain and sometimes with elaborate candelabras and gleaming silver cutlery. Barefoot, liveried bearers served course after course, moving in ghostly silence.

Menu for dinners at home

Soup

- Usually tomato soup (no one knew any other), served with three or four croutons

Main course

- *Methiji macchi* or
- *Bori chops* or
- *Kidney-liver bheja*

Accompaniments

- *Basmati rice* or
- *Moong dal* or
- *Besan kadhi*

Vegetables

- *Toori* or
- *Bharela bhindi* or
- *Karela stuffed with kheema*

Pudding

- Jelly and custard
- Rose/vanilla ice cream (flavouring imported from England). Ice cream was made at home in a wooden tub lined with ice and rock salt. Boiled-down milk was poured into a steel cylinder inserted into the tub, then churned by hand until it hardened.

    We children would peep through doors and windows, overawed by the sight.

    Dialmal, seeing what was happening in the affairs of the government, advised friends and relatives to begin searching for a safe refuge outside Sindh. However, most Sindhis were landowners and could not conceive of living any other way. They said, 'The man is getting old and does not know what he says. Leave hearth and home! Bah! The man is crazed and senile.' But seeing the state of affairs in Sindh from up close, Dialmal decided to set an example and establish a second home away from Sindh—a safe haven.

He first visited Bombay because one of his daughters and a niece had moved there after their wedding. He looked around for land but soon gave up the idea of moving to Bombay as war clouds loomed—World War II had begun—and the city, being a major port and the financial capital of the subcontinent, was deemed unsafe. He then went to Poona, but left disappointed, as it was too close to a metropolis like Bombay and he feared the children could be led astray. (Ironically, after Partition, my elder brother Hiroo would go on to study at Wadia College, Poona.)

Eventually, he took a journey to the interiors, to Madhya Pradesh with its capital at Indore, which had good schools and colleges and where the maharajas kept the city well administered. In a comparatively new colony, away from the centre of the city, he bought an acre of farmland, the produce of which would suffice for the family, and a six-room home with outhouses just across the road; and a dairy farm close by which could supply their daily milk requirement. The neighbours were friendly gentry who believed in simple living and high thinking. A financier, a doctor, a lawyer, a police inspector general, a hotelier, a teacher, a couple of businessmen and a college professor formed the small community.

Dialmal returned home a very satisfied person. Thenceforth, he and his wife would take a yearly trip to Indore, and stay there for a month or two. They would set up the home and keep the farm in order, engage reliable retainers for the establishments, and when he thought the farm will yield good results, he would return to Karachi.

Dialmal implored his only son to sell their ancestral land and start a new life, far from Sindh. The tragedy was that his own son refused, not that he did not believe his father but because the conditions at that time were not suitable for such a major move.

When Partition took place, everyone just took a few documents and some jewellery, locked their houses and went off on what they thought would be a short holiday across the border to visit relatives. No one imagined for a moment that there will be 'no return'. Little did they know that their houses would be broken into, and complete strangers would sleep in their beds!

Some of the people who occupied these palatial houses came from small villages across the border. They had never seen electric lights or ceiling fans. When they accidentally touched the switches, the lights came on and fans began to whirl. Not one of them knew how to switch them off. The faint of heart thought it was the spirits of the Hindus that had come to haunt them. Others braved the situation and tied thick ropes around the blades to stop the fans from turning, especially as winter had set in.

Hyderabad had an open drainage toilet-system. Villagers were used to going out into the fields for their ablutions and thought these were kitchens and burnt logs and did their cooking here.

Oh! A toilet for a kitchen!

08 Dewan Mulchand

As a young man, Dewan Mulchand started working for the Mir of Sindh as a *mukhtiarkar*. He was well versed in the Persian language and, as was the custom of the time, dressed like the Mir—loose trousers, a loose, long-sleeved shirt, a waistcoat and a tall cap like an inverted top hat.

The British, having heard of his excellence at work, offered him a prestigious position with higher remuneration. He declined, as by then his thoughts had turned towards spirituality. He dropped the prefix of Dewan and was thenceforth known as Bhai (the learned one). He was a Sanskrit scholar. It can be said he was a pioneer of Sanskrit studies in modern Sindh and his writings in Sindhi and Hindi were known throughout India.

Bhai Mulchand built a rustic structure in a park near his home, where bhajan-kirtan and religious discourses took place throughout the day. Bhajan-kirtan was always conducted in Sanskrit.

Many flocked to him to learn Sanskrit and study the scriptures. He was philanthropic to a fault, he owned not a penny. The men in the family—his brothers—decided to get better-paid jobs to meet the family's expenses and cater to Bhai's simple living and high thinking.

Dewan Sooratsingh became a *faujdar*, the highest position an Indian could hold in the police during the British Raj. As a reward for excellent service, the road across from his ancestral home was named Faujdari Lane and was known as such till Partition.

Dewan Doulatram became a leading lawyer in Sindh and

added to the coffers of the family, so that they could live in comfort.

The women of the house would constantly be stitching pyjamas and kurtas of broadcloth, one-size-fits-all, as they did not know when the Bhai would bring with himself someone in need of clothes.

Bhai Mulchand died penniless but was pious and blessed. The strip of land on which stood his hermit's hut was named Bhai Mulchand Lane. Many years later, his great-grandnephew, Dewan Gobindram, built their new ancestral home next to this.

Bhai Mulchand Lane was called such till about 1963.

09 Dewan Doulatram and The Big House

Dewan Doulatram had four sons. When the talk of inheritance started, Chandiram, the eldest, asked his father for the ancestral home as he had a family of 7-8 children and needed more accommodation to house them. Also, he was less educated than his younger brothers.

Doulatram conceded and also gave him part of the ancestral farmland for sustenance.

There was, however, one stipulation. A widowed aunt, who lived in quarters within the ancestral house, must not be disturbed, and Chandiram and his brothers would look after her needs. We called her Dadi Pavi and as a child I remember that all her meals would be sent from our house until we left Hyderabad.

Doulatram's own house across the street and bordering the church compound went to his youngest son Ramchand. Ramchand and his wife died at a very young age and his other brother Dialmal was given the house and all the responsibilities that went with it—his widowed mother, Ramchand's daughter and son, and the upkeep of the rustic cottage of Bhai Mulchand.

His third son, Dialmal, had by then qualified in law and become a judge, while his brother Gopaldas had joined the police service.

Doulatram's house was where Dialmal's son and two daughters grew up, as did Gopaldas's two sons and a daughter, alongside Ramchand's two children.

It was a real joint family. Gopaldas was frequently posted outside Hyderabad, and the cousins grew up together as brothers and sisters. This was a house of abundance. This was a house where everything was shared equally. This was a house where love ruled.

As the families expanded, there was a need for more space. Gobindram, the eldest of the cousins, was of marriageable age and a new house had to be built. The strip of garden to the west of Doulatram's house, bordering the church compound to the north, was acquired. Gobindram was given the task of dealing with the architects, approving and overseeing plans, and everything that goes into making a home.

He created a marvel of a house. Unique in plan and structure and quite apart from the run-of-the-mill houses of that time, which had a set pattern—a courtyard with a covered verandah leading to two rooms on one side and kitchen and bath and toilets on the other side. Hyderabad still had an open drainage system.

Dewan Gobindram had heard that there would be electricity in Hyderabad in a few years and so he installed electric wiring in anticipation. In 1926–27 Gobindram started the construction after several plans were drawn up and discarded and one was finally approved. Bhai Mulchand's cottage was not razed but left as it was and Gopaldas's house came up alongside it, facing the main road on one side and Bhai Mulchand Lane on the other.

To the north of Gopaldas's house was Gobindram's unit, with an interconnecting door. Adjoining Doulatram's house were the private quarters of Dialmal, where he could entertain male friends or attend to clients or matters of court. Being of a religious bent of mind, an upstairs room had also been built, which housed the Guru Granth Sahib and where religious rites were conducted and prasad made.

The central portion was huge, as big as a badminton court. This was my grandmother Haribai's domain. There were double doors throughout the house, so no mosquitoes or flies pestered

Nursery rhyme from Sindh

Paiso ladhum patta maan	Found one *paisa* on the ground
Paisay vartum ga-hu	With one paisa, I bought hay
Ga-hu dinam gain khe	I gave the hay to the cow
Gain dino kheer	The cow gave me milk
Kheer dinum amma khe	I gave the milk to my granny
Amma dino lolo	Granny gave me a *meetha lolo*
Lolo dinum kanv khe	I gave the lolo to the crow
Kanv dino khambh	The crow gave me a feather/quill
Khambh dinum Raja khe	I gave the quill to the King
Raja dino ghoro	The King gave me a horse
Chari ghum, chari ghum	I climbed on and rode the horse
Chandan phatako	Crazy crackers!
Jiye meenjo kako	Long live my uncle!
Kako vetho mar-ieh tey	Uncle sat on the stairs to the first floor
Vichoon dang-yus, dari-ah tey!	A scorpion crawled into his beard and bit him!

anyone. The daughters of the house and younger children were not allowed to go out or to eat outside food; everything they desired was made at home.

Everyone wished to come to our house as it was a party every day. It came to be known as 'The Big House'. We were one of the first to have *chiroli* on the ceiling, a plaster of Paris moulding of Lord Krishna dancing with his *gopis* in *raas*. Though there was only one Lord, each gopi believed he was dancing solely with her. Such a colourful display—enough to lull you into a mesmerized slumber.

10 The Joint Family

Havelis have given way to cubbyhole flats, as the joint family has broken down into nuclear families. The houses of yore were huge and divided into several units for the families of married sons to lead their own lives. The only consistent factor was the kitchen. It was common to all, and everyone was expected to partake of their meals together. Their guiding principle was: 'The family that eats together, stays together.' It was here, at the dinner table, that all family matters were discussed and sorted out, be it children's education, a vacation, a marriage, business or finances.

Cousins were considered brothers, and nothing was kept secret from any family member. There were many fights amongst the children and jealousies amongst the elders, yet the household ran smoothly.

All the sons gave their earnings to the family Grand Dame, who doled out the monies according to the need of each one in the family; besides keeping aside a major portion for the running of the household.

'Parties', as such, were unheard of. There were so many people in the house that there was no need for any outsiders. Every day was a party.

The children's or elders' friends who visited would be given at least *paapar-pani*. Of course the pani would be no less than a glass of sherbet. Depending on the status of the person or the frequency of the visits, tikkis, samosas or bhajjias would be served, accompanied by *lumlet*, as the old ladies called Nusserwanji's sunny yellow aerated lemonade.

Old scores were forgotten and life was great.

It would sound scandalous in today's world if there were three or four eating sessions at one meal. The men of the house were served first. They were waited on hand and foot and served the choicest of foods, be it vegetarian or non-vegetarian, as they were the earning members and had to remain in good health.

Next came the children, the darlings of the family, who used their brains at school. Then it was the turn of the ladies of the family, the grown-up daughters and the daughters-in-law. Even though they were on call day and night, they were thought not to need so much energy. And finally, it was Amma, the Grand Dame of the household, who took her meal last.

11 Peel Pawas

The modern concept of a complete bedroom is one that has side tables. They serve both a purpose and a utility. Now that we have access to electricity, a pretty table lamp can complement the décor of the room. At the touch of a button, we can now satisfy our desires of reading when we please—late at night or early in the morning, when natural light is not sufficient. Now the children study well into the night to prepare for their exams.

I remember that my elder brother and I never set an alarm. He used to like studying late into the night, whereas I used to prefer the quiet of the early morning. So at whatever time he chose to close his books, three o'clock or four o'clock, he would wake me up and at the touch of a button my room would be flooded with light.

A glass of water or a flask of tea or coffee can easily find a place on the side table. A pad and pen to jot down things to do the next day, or maybe a medicine box to help induce sleep or ease aches and pains experienced through the day. The bedside table indeed has its uses.

There are various designs to suit individual preferences: three drawers with a common shutter to lock away things from prying eyes, or a taller table with one drawer and an open shelf for easy access to reading material.

These days, the 'wood' has changed. One hears of ply, block board and veneers, which need constant maintenance. Of course, there is also the option of melamine, which leaves no marks on the surface—or glass, marble or granite—the choices are vast.

In the good old days when there was no electricity but only candles, kerosene lamps and later, hurricane lanterns, one adhered to sayings like 'early to bed and early to rise, makes a man healthy, wealthy and wise'. Rightly so, as everyone got sufficient sleep and woke up refreshed to face the new day.

In the old days, furniture was made from termite-free seasoned woods like teak, cedar, ebony, mahogany and sandalwood, prized for their natural grain and sheen. Just a dash of polish with linseed oil and it looked new for ever and ever.

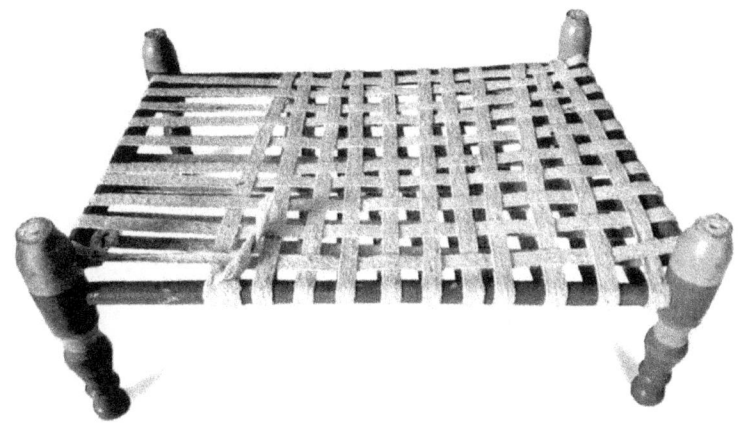

A toy replica of a Sindhi charpoy

Every bride used to get a wardrobe with a mirror and a built-in secret drawer in which to store her jewels—her *streedhan*, a four-poster bed and a sewing machine, the latter a gift from an elder sister. The bed had four thick, sturdy *pawas*, which were beautifully carved or crafted on a lathe. At the top of each leg was a built-in box in which the young lady could store buttons, bows, hair clips, medicines or scratch pads. All four pawas were connected by thick wooden supports, which were interwoven with a three- to four-inch-wide cotton *navaar*. This formed the base on which the bedding was laid. Every seven to eight days, the domestic workers would tighten the navaar while making the beds.

The frame's supports were so thick and firm that they came to be known as *peel pawa*.

The phrase later became synonymous with a woman's thick, muscular legs and if such a sight was seen, one would remark, 'Look at her peel pawas!'

12. The Neem Tree

In the days of Peg-Leg Pete, the treasure chart might have read, 'A hundred yards to the south of the church stands a *neem* tree with sweet yellow berries, and 10 feet deep lies the treasure chest.'

I don't know how or whose treasure was buried there. Stories of pirates were told 'as those coming by ship'. A more likely place would have been Karachi, as it was a seaport. Then why Hyderabad?

By then, the house had been built and the neem tree stood on Father's property—as did whatever lay under it. The British came first, in search of the treasure, and asked for permission to dig around the tree. Father struck a deal with them that if such a treasure was found, his share would be 50 per cent plus the area dug up would have to be restored. They agreed. Father informed them that, when the foundation of the house was laid, they had already dug more than 10 feet deep and found nothing.

But the British were not deterred. The digging started but nothing was found. Maybe the constant movement of the earth had shifted the chest from its original position?

After the British came the Dutch and then the Portuguese, but Father refused to have anything to do with them as the inconvenience was far greater than the pleasure of possessing a treasure. He suggested to them that they examine the ground near the Indus river where, on a nearby hillock, stood another church. And what of the neem tree with the sweet yellow berries? No such tree could be found in the vicinity of that church, which was deserted, except for the feathered company.

As they say, 'hope springs eternal in the human breast'. After Partition maybe the treasure made its way to China and now the Chinese and the Pakistanis can share the booty!

13 The Anglo-Indians

The Anglo-Indians came to be known thus after World War II.

In India, the Christian community intermarried with British soldiers, commonly known as Tommies. Although their rank was low, the pay was good, and since there was no such thing as an arranged match within the community, girls had to find their own partners. The Tommy offered them a good lifestyle. Such unions, however, were forbidden for Hindu girls who were brought up in conservative families. Even though many were convent-educated, they did not have the freedom of stepping out of the house unescorted.

A new word was coined and the children of such alliances came to be known as Anglo-Indians. They were fair of face and liberated. They thought they were way above the Hindu community and considered themselves more British than the British themselves.

Hindus derogatorily referred to them as *chhi-chhis*, meaning soiled, or as *char-annis* meaning four annas. In other words, they were considered 75 per cent Indian and only 25 per cent English.

They were a bold community. Wild in their ways, with not a care in the world for criticism of any kind. It cannot be said that they were highly educated or even wanted to be, whereas the Hindu children aspired to be engineers, doctors, lawyers or go abroad—mainly to England—to be barristers.

The girls would graduate from school and often take up courses in shorthand and typing to become secretaries. They were hard-working and made excellent assistants to their English bosses. Their fluency in English got them highly paid jobs.

The boys' ambitions were mostly to join the railways. After passing out of school, a Senior Cambridge degree being the minimum requirement, fluency in reading and writing and an understanding of the English language stood them in good stead. While waiting for even an engine driver's job, they would go to the railway yard to learn the nitty-gritty of the steam engine. An engine driver's job was considered prestigious and held a lot of clout within the railway echelons. They were highly paid, the perquisites were attractive, they were given living quarters ('I live at railway quarters' was considered a good address), paid leave, and medical and travel compensation for the family.

There were two boys in my class—Lenny and Kenny—who were very bright and could have qualified for any professional degree and estimable practice/job. But no, the lure of making good money at an early age drew them to the railways.

Apart from this, the Anglo-Indians would take up bit roles as 'extras' in films as they had the skills and no inhibitions about singing, dancing, smoking, drinking or frivolous dressing.

14 Bombay Delights

My very first visit to Bombay was in the year 1942. I was a little girl, not yet twelve, and thrilled to take a trip out of Hyderabad. It was an early present for my thirteenth birthday. After a very disciplined upbringing, I thought it would be great fun to be on my own, without the supervision of elders. Dad's friend was taking a vacation with his family, and I was booked in the same train compartment.

In those days, the railways were the most popular mode of transport to distant places. It took 2–3 days to travel from from Hyderabad to Bombay. The compartments had curtains on the windows, a folding table and chair that could be used for writing or having meals, and an easy chair on which one could recline, rest and relax. There was also an attached bath and toilet to freshen up during the journey. Once the compartment was reserved, no other person could make use of it during the day or night allotted.

After copious tears at the station—since I had never been away from home—and goodbyes to family and friends, the train set off from Hyderabad station for Bombay, the city lights of the metropolis only spoken about until then. Daddy had friends along the whole route and we were provided with hot meals for breakfast, lunch, tea and dinner.

My aunt Devaki came to receive me at the station and took me to her home at Jenkins House on Henry Road, off Colaba Causeway (the building still stands in all its glory, though the tenants have since changed). I looked forward to my stay with her. The Causeway was a delight. Shops with breathtaking window displays lined even, clean pavements. One could walk the length of the Causeway under the arches, protected from the vagaries of the weather. There were no ramshackle stalls, no hawkers or beggars vying with each other for space on the footpaths. The city felt as safe as a home.

People from all over the world came to Bombay—the financial capital of India. Everything was so neat and clean. The streets used to be washed in the wee hours of the morning. The public at large was always well dressed, and even strangers were courteous to each other. Words like 'please', 'thank you' and 'sorry' were like a second skin. Cinema halls such as Regal, Eros and Metro were fully carpeted, and Sundays at the movies were like a fashion show. Everyone was dressed quite literally in their Sunday best.

There were no high-rises. All the buildings on Marine Drive were symmetrical six-storey structures in the art deco style, and elsewhere in the city, buildings were generally three- to four-storey walk-ups.

From Malabar Hill's Hanging Gardens, one could see a row of lights from Government House to Back Bay. It looked like a necklace, as it traced the curve of the bay. In fact, it was known as the Queen's Necklace because of the single row of gaslights that twinkled like blue diamonds.

The short gaslight posts were tended by *gaswallahs* who would walk the distance before sundown, carrying long poles with a hook at the end to pull up the lever, release the gas, light it and voilà! The Queen's Necklace would shimmer and shine, without any ugly hoardings and advertisement boards to hinder such a wondrous view. At dawn, the gas men would make the same journey to extinguish the lights so that the Sun God, Surya, could shower His light and warmth on the city.

The houses had sloping roofs covered with red clay tiles, called *kavelu*, so that during the monsoon—the *chowmasa* or the four months of heavy rain—rainwater flowed off the rooftops and there was no leakage inside. Just before the monsoon, young lads carrying buckets of liquid tar and a broom would call out, '*dambar lagaalo*', i.e. touch up with tar to seal off all cracks and crevices on the roofs. Very much like London's chimney sweeps.

Those are the sounds of the city one misses. It was like music to the ears. Now, it is harsh sounds of horns and revving buses, cars and motorbikes.

The Gateway of India at Apollo Bunder was a popular promenade. The famous Taj Mahal Hotel and its annexe, the Greens Hotel, stood as silent sentinels guarding the Gateway.

Dhanraj Mahal, another beautiful stone structure at Apollo Bunder, had a famous salon on its premises—The House of Max Factor. My aunt took me there and, as another preteen present, bought me a make-up box. I was on cloud nine! She did not stop at that. She asked the beautician to style my hair and teach me how to use the make-up kit. This was the very first time that I used lipstick, rouge and pancake make-up. What a thrill it was! I could hardly recognize myself and could not help but gaze at the vision in the mirror.

Like in the childhood fairy tale, I felt like saying, 'Mirror, mirror on the wall, who is the fairest of them all?' And of course, I expected to hear, 'Sarla, thou art the fairest of them all!' To top it all, I was treated to an evening at the Cricket Club of India. The manicured expanse of its lawns and the huge clubhouse were nothing like what we had in Hyderabad.

I felt like a princess. But as all good things must come to an end, Auntie creamed off all my makeup as soon as we reached home and I turned into Simple Sarla once again—Cinderella amongst the ashes.

15. Mirs and Dr Manghanmal

Sindh was well known for its powerful zamindars. The Hindu zamindars treated their staff with decency, paid them well, were humane towards them, and took care of their every need, but were also firm with them, as was required by a zamindar. The Muslim zamindars, on the other hand, were more like feudal lords whose word was law. Their staff feared them and never questioned them, much like thakurs or dons of today's world.

They would subject not only the women in their service but also the women of their own households—be it their mothers, sisters, daughters or cousins—to do their bidding. In India, a woman is worshipped, be she literate or illiterate, whereas for the Muslim zamindar, a woman was regarded as mere chattel.

The only excuse the ladies of such households had if they wanted to take in some air was to complain of imaginary ills and go see a doctor. Orthodox Muslim families of pre-Partition India often preferred Hindu doctors, who were gentle in their manners and respectful towards womenfolk—unlike the men of the house, who were respectful only to their Muslim doctors.

Dr Manghanmal had many stories to tell. He was a leading doctor in Hyderabad, and many of the *mirs* who lived in palaces would send for him. One such family once called him. He was a young man then; handsome and well spoken. The mir took him to the zenana, the section of the house where the ladies were kept in strict purdah. The lady in question had a high fever. The doctor was given only a two by two inch portion of her wrist and asked to diagnose what was wrong with her.

The doctor did some quick thinking. He first put his two

fingers on her wrist, felt her burning with fever, then started counting her pulse rate which, of course, confirmed she had fever. To earn his fee, he took some time as if to show that the lady was seriously ill. Knowing that these poor rich women were prisoners in their own homes, he advised Shah Sahib to bring her to the clinic where he could take an X-ray of her chest to rule out any lung infection.

Shah Sahib would have none of it, but the doctor told him the next step would be tuberculosis and she would be no good to anyone. Shah Sahib ultimately consented but with a condition. The doctor was to carry out the examination at night, after clinic hours, and no member of the doctor's staff was to be present. The doctor could not touch the lady but could give instructions and he would be blindfolded as the *mirzadi* would be without a burqa.

All went according to the mir's instructions. Of course the doctor was right—she had chest congestion. Medicine was prescribed and the lady was soon up and about! After that Shah Sahib would allow the ladies of the household to go to the clinic when all the patients had left. The ladies often feigned an illness just to get out of the house.

Soon after this episode, the feudal lord of a nearby village knocked on the doctor's door in the wee hours of the morning. The whole household was woken up from deep slumber, so loud was the knocking. When the doctor opened the door, he saw Shah Sahib in a sweat and his horse foaming at the mouth. The doctor was taken aback and asked, 'What is the matter and how can I help you?' The man answered, 'I have ridden hard all night and I am sick and exhausted.'

The doctor took him into the clinic adjoining the house, calmed him down with a glass of water and examined him. 'Shah Sahib, there is nothing seriously wrong; you have a fever and you are tired. Here is a prescription, just take these pills and in a couple of days you will be right as rain.'

But the Shah Sahib said, 'Doctor, I have to appear in court today at 10 a.m. and I require a certificate to say that I have not left my bed since the last four days.' The doctor immediately sensed foul play and replied, 'Shah Sahib, I cannot do that but I can modify my statement and certify that you have been under my care since yesterday. It is against medical ethics to do otherwise, more so since this is a court case.'

The Shah left the clinic without uttering a word. The doctor knew he had lost a good, well-paying patient. The next day he came to know that the Shah had murdered a zamindar four days ago—hence the request for a backdated medical certificate.

Evidently the Shah must have paid some other doctor a good deal of money for a false certificate. He was acquitted of the murder charge due to insufficient evidence. The benefit of the doubt saved the Shah from the gallows and the good sense and honesty of the doctor from a besmirched career.

16 The Journey of No Return

The year was 1947. Trouble was brewing in India. The Britishers knew that the time had come when they must leave. Talks and meetings with the British—between Lord Mountbatten (the first Governor General of India), Mahatma Gandhi, Jawaharlal Nehru and Muhammad Ali Jinnah—were underway, but the British were loath to leave their Crown Jewel, India, in peace, and ultimately the subcontinent was divided into India and Pakistan.

My elder brother Hiroo was a sea scout, as were several other young boys from Amil Colony No. 2—a posh residential area of Karachi, where mostly Amil gentry lived. In those days, a bungalow's terrace room was generally allotted to the eldest son of the family.

There were whispered talks about how Muslims would kidnap the *hooris* of Sindh, beautiful Amil Hindu girls whom they likened to angels and fairies of paradise. Many times, in the middle of the night, I would wake up with a start on hearing screams of protest and cries for help. It was so frightening.

The young scouts decided not to be caught napping. They stocked their terraces with empty glass bottles, bric-a-brac, any and every discarded object that could be used as a missile.

As sea scouts, they were well versed in Morse code. They sectioned off the area, organized groups and kept vigil through the night, keeping contact by Morse code and ready to respond at a moment's notice.

This went on till 14 August 1947, when most families decided to leave Sindh for some time or at least send their young girls out of the country till matters quietened down. Most Amils, even though they were in good jobs, were of course also landowners. They thought they will take their families, cash, jewellery and documents, leave them in safe custody and return.

Little did they know that there will be no return. Their lands were taken, standing crops sold off, houses looted and illegally occupied, and the Pakistani government turned a Nelson's eye to all that went on. The motto became: 'What you grab, register as your own!'

As a young teenager, I had read Leon Uris's *Exodus*. At the time, I think I understood very little of it. Its full meaning struck me only years later when friends and relatives—myself included—had to leave our homeland. The worldly goods, the attachments, the memories, the heart and soul of hearth and home—all was lost, as also our motherland—Sindh—to the Muslims who, until then, had never dared to enter any town in Sindh, but lived in ghettos in the interiors, unlettered.

The displaced Sindhis were accommodated in camps across India, in unhygienic conditions. They desired a place they could call Sindh but their appeals fell on deaf ears. From *raja* to *runk*—such was their fate.

Education suffered. Now it became a matter of survival. And with the motto 'Never say die! Up man, and try', they bounced back.

The women would make delicacies and the men would go and sell them. They would identify Sindhi families already settled in the city and offer them their wares. There was not a Sindhi who would beg, and they always returned the correct change.

After 61 years of Independence, on 26 June 2008, the Government of India gave those who still lived in the Ulhasnagar refugee camps ownership of the land on which they lived, allowing them to develop and make homes for themselves. I have seen one such camp developed in Baroda (now Vadodara). From a low-lying marshy land, it has been turned into a beautiful haven.

Delicacies made in the Sindhi camps

The most popular was *murmulan-ji-mithai,* a kind of sweet made from *murmala.* Milk was boiled down to half its quantity, the murmala was put into it with sugar and aromatic spices. There was no *mawa* in those days.

There was also *pistan-ji-mithai, nariyal-ji-mithai, badaam-pistajo varo.* The women in the Sindhi camps also sold pickles of all kinds, the favourite being mango, then lemon, button onions, carrots.

17 The Hooris of Sindh

The Partition of India took place on 15 August 1947, and I was out of Karachi on 6 September 1947. My maternal uncle, Dada Chander, owned a dry dock in Karachi, where ships could be repaired and made seaworthy. A liner from Australia made a stop at the dockyard for repairs. Dada happened to mention this at the dinner table. At such troubled times, this was like a godsend, a one-in-a-million chance to get all the young girls out of the troubled country to the safety of India.

Sindhi Amil girls were considered pretty and stylish, and Sindhi Muslims always said, 'We will kidnap the hooris of Sindh.' The Amil community implored Dada Chander to ask the ship's captain if he would take such a 'precious cargo'.

The captain declined. He said the stop at Karachi was unforeseen and imperative as the ship needed repairs urgently, otherwise he had no authority to stop at any Oriental port. In view of the situation, the captain was asked to take permission from his office in Australia to make a slight detour and take as many young girls as he could accommodate to Bombay. Permission was granted. Other passengers were informed of the delay in reaching their respective destinations, and the hooris of Sindh left for Bombay; carrying with them the family jewels and important documents to a safe haven. Most of the girls, young brides and pregnant ladies, left for Bombay under the pretext of visiting family and friends, not realizing that they will never again see their homeland.

We were the fortunate ones who had friends to look after us. I cannot recollect who my co-passengers were as this was my first trip on board a ship, and I was so seasick that I did not leave my cabin. Also, the sorrow of separation from my parents put me into a deep depression. Sita Shivdasani (who later became my sister-in-law), Dada Hassa Shivdasani and Bhabhi Radhi, his very elegant wife, came to receive me at the docks.

Those who were inland, i.e. in Hyderabad and other districts, had to rely on the railways. Most of them just crossed the border and settled down in Kutch, Bhuj, Gujarat and other places in the Bombay Presidency. Many had nowhere to go. They were looted at the stations and the border guards of Pakistan became rich overnight. Some came only in the clothes they had on them and had to survive in refugee camps hastily set up by the Government of India. A family of five would be given only one blanket, one tin mug and one tin plate. Whether they used it for ablutions or as a drinking vessel was no one's concern. Families were often separated from each other and if enquiries were made with the concerned officer, he would fly into a temper, little realizing that these were people who had given up everything so that the Indian side of the country could celebrate.

The camps were damp, dark and dirty, most of them on swampy land. Young girls had to go long distances to use the common toilets. Malaria and diarrhoea were rampant but the will of the Sindhis and Punjabis was strong. Their motto, as mentioned earlier, was 'Never say die! Up man, and try.' Music united the families and brought smiles to their lips. They were a hard-working people and no work was below their dignity. I think that is what made Mahatma Gandhi to coin the phrase 'Work is worship'.

Sindhi women were skilled in embroidery, stitching (an age-old custom was that when a young girl got married, the older married sister would gift her a sewing machine), and making sweetmeats, sherbets and pickles. So came about a cottage industry in the camps. The women would make delicacies, and the husbands and sons would go out and sell them at nominal prices.

As demand grew, so did the variety and price of the products. The smaller children would go out in groups to nearby railway stations and sell homemade candy, pocket combs, pencils. If customers had no change and the children were told to 'keep the change', it would touch them on the raw, and the latter would reply, 'I am selling goods and not begging. I will be here at the same place and you can make good on the money.'

From the bottom of the graph they rose, unschooled but successful businessmen, professionals and philanthropists to boot. Today, some of the best schools, colleges, hospitals in Bombay have been started by Sindhis. I have never known a Sindhi to say 'I can't do this'. The word 'can't' does not exist in their dictionary. Nor would they ever say 'This is below my dignity.' Their heads have always been held high.

18 Transvestites

I got married in Bombay on 12 December 1952 and left for Hyderabad, Sindh, in Pakistan, on 4 January 1953 as my husband Dr Nari had to report for duty on 5 January 1953 at the Civil Hospital there.

As a young bride, I hardly had time to reflect on what life in Pakistan—a Muslim country where most women lived in purdah or wore a burqa—might be like. I had no friends there. Everyone in India thought I was quite mad to accept Pakistan as my new home. By then, I was used to the wide open spaces and the freedom of India, where girls could move freely and safely, even after sundown.

The greatest attraction was that my parents were in Karachi, just one and a half hours by train from Hyderabad. Bombay had seemed inaccessible from Karachi!

Amongst the Sindhi Hindus of Hyderabad, eunuchs were unheard of, but in India, both Hindus and Muslims would see them arrive at their doorsteps during weddings and births. They would sing and dance, give their blessings—which was considered a good omen, accept their *baksheesh* and leave.

I was not used to all this. As a matter of fact, I did not even know who or what a transvestite was and had never seen one. As children we had heard stories of them as half men and half women who kidnapped babies, and we were always terrified of them.

When we reached Hyderabad, word spread that the young doctor was bringing home a bride. The next morning, five to six strapping eunuchs arrived and demanded to see the bride. My living quarters were on the first floor, and when my mother-in-law bade her son and me to come down I thought it was a call for breakfast.

Imagine my shock at seeing these men/women or *chhakkas*, as they are locally called. I was terrified and hid behind my mother-in-law, clutching my husband's arm. But none of the eunuchs took any notice of me. They were expecting a sari-clad, bejewelled, coy girl with her head covered and anklets tinkling. I had shed my shimmering bridal clothes for a comfortable shirt and trousers. When they did not hear the rustle of flowing clothes or the tinkling of *panzebs*, they again asked, 'Doctor Sahib, where is the *dulhan*, the bride?'

Nari stepped back so that I could be viewed, the object of their curiosity, and said, 'Here she is,' indicating me, the trouser-clad young girl. No *mehendi*, no *maang-tikka*, no anklets. It did not register with them that a new bride would be dressed as a boy. It's a good thing they did not mistake me for one of their own and abduct me! Nari took out a wad of notes and said, 'Here is your baksheesh, give your blessings and be on your way as I am getting late for my duty at the hospital.'

With my husband Dr Nari Kripalani on our wedding day on 12 December 1952

They were aghast that this trouser-clad girl could be the bride, but they got what they had come for and left murmuring and whispering amongst themselves.

The next time I saw them was when my son was born. He was the first grandchild and the first boy who had graced the family after 26 years i.e. the first boy to be born after Dr Nari. The whole of Hyderabad celebrated and the eunuchs sang and danced and entertained. My father-in-law, Dr Manghanmal, gave money to them generously.

They came back when I had my daughter, again the first granddaughter who was born under favourable stars. A Friday's child, loving and giving, she made her appearance at 6.30 a.m., just as the Eid aazan was announced. The road outside our house was blocked by thousands of devotees saying their Eid prayers. Catholics all over the world were also observing Good Friday. My father-in-law stopped the eunuchs from leaving. They said in a wise tone, a girl is also welcome, may the Lord bless her.

My father-in-law replied, 'This is my only granddaughter. She is our Laxmi—the Goddess of Wealth—and more precious than a boy, so I will give you twofold.' They were delighted because normally they received nothing for the birth of a girl. They departed in good cheer, leaving us with laughter and their blessings for the little girl.

19 Hyderabad, Banaras and Dr Nari

My husband Dr Nari's clinic was situated at Mian-Fakir-Jo-Pir, or Reshmi Gulley, as it was called after Partition.

He was tall, dark and handsome, and had pleasant bedside manners. He had a 'thinking' head on his shoulders, hence he was very popular amongs this patients.

After the Partition of India, the Muslim families patronized Hindu doctors more than their Muslim counterparts, as they knew that the Hindus would not look lustfully at their womenfolk (as if they were impotent) but treat them courteously. So, the rich and poor flocked to Hindu doctors.

Dr Nari's clinic was not far from the red-light area of Hyderabad, and he was often asked to make house calls at the pleasure houses, which he attended after his clinic hours, late in the evenings. I always knew about these visits, for on his return, when he handed me the day's earnings, the notes would carry the fragrance of attar that the nautch girls used. The scent of attar lingers for a longer time, and is sharper than that of the perfume that the ladies of fashion use.

He would tell me many stories of those beautiful girls who were enticed into the flesh trade. The so-called high society women would look down their noses at them and talk in whispers about these nautch girls who were invited by their menfolk for entertainment on special occasions. In spite of their attitude, whenever the ladies got a chance, they would not hesitate to momentarily admire the girls; swirling and shaking in their colourful and dazzling dresses and tapping their toes in rhythm to the *ghungroos* and singing in dulcet tones to the *wah-wah* of their male audience.

Dr Nari knew about their trials and tribulations and pitied them. He would talk to them, advise them and try to alleviate their sorrows.

One such house call took him to the doorstep of Hoorbai. He examined her and prescribed appropriate medication. Just as he was about to leave, she beckoned him into an anteroom. The doctor did not know how to react! Being a Hindu, he was slightly apprehensive about entering the inner quarters of a gharara-clad Muslim woman, even though she was a call girl. His car and driver were waiting to take him home. The Muslim driver knew that his master did not normally take longer than 20–30 minutes on such a visit. What would he think? What about the others in the chawl?

In a flash, all these thoughts crossed his mind, for which he had no answers. On entering the anteroom, Hoorbai drew aside a curtain behind which was a cupboard full of statuettes of gold, silver, crystal, clay, glass, metal, *meenakari*, gem-studded, painted (you name it, she had it), of all the Hindu gods and goddesses. It was breathtaking! A sight worth seeing!

'Doctor,' she said, 'this secret has lived with me ever since I came to Hyderabad, Pakistan. Nobody knows about it. When I feel sad, I come here and pray. I keep this locked at all times. Now that I am getting old, I was yearning to share it with someone I could trust...'

This is what she related... 'I was a beautiful, carefree young girl. The only child born to a high-caste Brahmin family in Banaras. Much pampered by all. From my early childhood I would accompany my parents to temples and sing bhajans. I was very fond of singing and dancing.

'Sometime in my teens, I fell in with wrong, nay, bad

company. I rebelled against my parents. The dance lessons they had so innocently arranged for me became the foundation of a nautch girl's training. I was ostracized by family and friends. After Partition I wanted to stay back in Banaras but my family refused to accept me and I had no option but to accompany my Muslim friends to Hyderabad, Sindh.

'My birth name is Hira—a diamond. That sparkling diamond Hira became Hoorbai, a nautch girl. The mother or the dame of our camp was good to me and because of my background kept me away from the flesh trade. Many were the *mujras* I performed for the aristocracy—at births and weddings—and earned a goodly sum for the mother to sustain her in her old age. Now at the end of my life, I do penance and ask forgiveness from my God and my parents.

'Oh Banaras, how I miss thee. The tinkling of temple bells and the *aartis* on the banks of Ganga maiya, the vast and *vishal* holy river, where I wish I could take a dip and wash away my sins.'

20 Dewan Gobindram and Narayan

My father, Dewan Gobindram, stayed on in Karachi after Partition. He moved from a bungalow on Clayton Road, Amil Colony No. 2, to a flat near Laurence Quarter in a Parsi colony. It was a rented house on the first floor. Our landlord, Mr Jimmy Sethna, occupied the ground floor. With all the family having migrated to India, my father felt safer here amongst friends. He believed my mother would be more secure here, especially when he had to go to Jacobabad to oversee his land and farm.

The Americans have now built a modern airport at Jacobabad. But at the time of Partition, my father had to make an arduous two-day journey from Karachi in the south to Jacobabad in the north of Sindh, where he would be met by his foreman and his horse-drawn carriage to take him to his farm, which was another hour's journey by road.

The foreman, Narayan, had come into my father's

Dewan Gobindram Dialmal

service as a nine-year-old orphan. My father educated him, gave him a job, bought him a house in Jacobabad, got him married, and helped raise and educate his children. He was considered part of an extended family and was my father's right-hand man.

Then came the Partition of India and Pakistan and the peace-loving people of Sindh experienced fear for the first time.

Narayan heard that Grandpa and Grandma were taking Gobindram's children across the border. He wished to accompany them with his entire family. Father told him, 'Narayan, I am still here. The children are going as they will lose an academic year. Moreover, in these uncertain times, we don't know how the "settling-in" will take place, and the house isn't large enough to accommodate so many people, or feed so many. The rationing system has also been introduced.

'Besides, Jacobabad is still very safe and there is no strife between Hindus and Muslims. I promise you, the day my wife and I leave, your whole family will leave with us.'

Narayan kept quiet but secretly tracked our whereabouts and left his master in the lurch. In the year that Grandpa passed away, in 1950, early one morning, we found him on our doorstep in Indore. My grandma was flabbergasted, then angry, and declined his salutation of touching her feet and refused to bless him.

Grandpa had just passed away, and the responsibility of the family had fallen on her shoulders. He had bought the house and a small farm in the vicinity—just enough for the survival of the family.

Narayan wanted to be reinstated as the foreman of the farm and settle down in Indore with his family. But Grandma would have none of it. She told him so in no uncertain words. 'You left my only son and daughter-in-law without their permission, when they have been so generous to you since you were nine. I can no longer trust you. I will not throw out those who are working with me and have been faithful to me.' Narayan had thought Grandma would welcome him with open arms. He must have been very disappointed.

Grandma, though unlettered—she was married at the age of nine or ten—was the best accountant. To look after a household of school- and college-going children and a farm was no small task. She was a respected senior citizen, well known in Indore for her generosity. No Sindhi refugee was turned away from her door. No matter what someone was selling, she will buy something.

By then my younger aunt's in-laws' family had also found their way to Indore, and the annexe of the house was given to them. Grandma very amicably settled quarrels between the children and the in-laws. The latter demanded attention and felt they should be living in the main house. Here, she was very firm. The children cannot be dislodged as they needed their space to study.

It must have been such a trial to keep a smile on her face and pacify the in-laws. She would go out of her way to give them fresh vegetables from the farm while the rest of the household had to eat what the vendor offered.

In those days of 'rationing', the farm owners had to give up a quota of wheat to get just one small loaf of bread. Since the children were used to an English breakfast, she would keep the bread for them on weekdays. On Sundays the bread would be given to the in-laws and Grandma would make a special breakfast for the children, even if all three requested something different.

The children were unaware of the ache in her heart—the pain for her son and daughter-in-law in Karachi, and the fate of the children if something happened to her. Yet, the smile on her face always welcomed everyone.

Sarla as a teenager in Karachi.

Short Stories of Others in Sindh

21 Prabha

I was born on 8 October 1941 and was six years old when Partition took place. I have two sisters and a brother; my younger sister was born in India.

My father had four sisters and one brother—all well married and settled in Lahore, as was he. We lived in the Mozang locality, which was interspersed with Muslim families who were quite friendly.

My maternal grandfather's home was in Shallu Mohalla, Lahore. His next-door neighbour was the well-known singer and actress Noorjehan and when we, as children, visited our maternal family, we would feel thrilled that a celebrity lived next door.

Even though Shallu Mohalla was a predominantly Hindu area, the surrounding houses belonged to Muslims.

By then, migration had already started in Punjab. People from across the border were coming in hordes, and their attitude was anti-Hindu. Having seen the looting they also desired to get whatever they could for free. Actually, the first ones to snatch and grab were the poorest of the poor from small villages who probably lived in mud huts and had nothing to lose, regardless of where they ended up.

Our Muslim friends advised us to go away to family or friends or at least send away the womenfolk till things settled down.

We locked the house and left for the station as if we were just going out for the day. My mother wore as much jewellery as she could, as she did not want to stand out or show that we were leaving the country. Everything, but everything, was left behind, for we were never to return.

We boarded a train to Delhi, where some relatives had settled before Partition. It was too much to ask for sustenance for a whole family as in those days no matter how small a house, the joint family lived together and could hardly be expected to house another large family.

On board the train, it was chaos. At every station Muslims would board the train and seek out Hindus, and pull them off the train. We children were asked to hide under the berths. My father and his brother were asked to hide in the toilets or jump off the still-moving train as it neared a station, and then to jump back on once it left the station. My paternal grandfather and his two brothers were brutally killed within our sight and we could do nothing. Fear was written on every face. No one realized it would be so bad.

At last, we reached Delhi. There were many volunteers who took us to a refugee camp. We were registered and allotted one small room. There were no toilets and we had to perform our ablutions in the open. Then came the long queues for food. We were given 5 kg of substandard grain, 5 kg of barley, 5 kg of wheat and some chana dal per person per month. How we cooked it was our problem.

Again we had to queue up for hours to get a utensil. The only thing in plenty was clean drinking water. Punjab, with its many rivers, gave us plenty of water but we needed vessels to store that water. By then, winter had set in, and there were no warm clothes. We had to queue up for five to six hours for the one blanket allotted to one family. Those were sorry times.

Our uncles in Delhi were contacted. They were building contractors, Mr Deshraj Luthra and his partner Mr Mangaldas Verma. As they were moving to Bombay, which was emerging as a business hub, and had acquired land near Tansa Lake, which they were asked to develop; they offered my father a job and asked him to move there. We moved out of the refugee camp and reached Bombay. They put up a factory at Sewri and, along with the job, gave my father quarters to house his family. After that there was no looking back. I enrolled in Hindi High School in Ghatkopar and then graduated from Guru Nanak Khalsa College. Then I got a job as a teacher in Shri Gauridutt Mittal Vidyalaya. Later, I went on to become the headmistress of the junior school.

 I am happily married now. I have a married daughter in New Bombay (now Navi Mumbai), a granddaughter who is a practising dentist and a son who works for Mahindra's. All is well that ends well.

22   Vijay Kapoor

I was nine years old at the time of Partition. My family consisted of Father, Mother and two older brothers. We lived in Subhash Nagar, Lahore, and had not a care in the world. Subhash Nagar was basically a Hindu mohalla of 60–70 families and some Muslim households who lived in peace. As a matter of fact, we never felt any different from each other. My father was a dealer in electrical goods and we lived comfortably.

At this particular time he had gone to Delhi with his partner to make purchases and had left the itinerary with Mother since there were no mobiles for prompt communication. Lahore was already teeming with migrants from across the border. They needed a place to live and the easiest way was to kill Hindus and usurp their homes and businesses.

On that fateful night, about a hundred Muslims came into our area and would have massacred all of us had our Muslim friends not called the military. We were saved! On the morrow, our neighbours advised us to leave because the next time we may not be lucky enough to tell the tale.

There was a loyal local tongawallah, a Muslim, who said that come what may, he would take us to the railway station.

The next day, Mother took as much jewellery as possible, locked the house, and—on that hot June day in 1947—left home with her three sons aged 13, 11, and 9, never to return.

We had relatives in Kullu and decided to go there and wait for Father. Kullu was about a 14–15-hour journey from Lahore, and it seemed the right place to go to. The good tongawallah, true to his word, covered his tonga with a cloth as if he was ferrying burqa-clad Muslim ladies and got us safely to the station.

From there, we travelled to Kullu to stay at my *masi*'s place. We stayed there for six months and then joined our father in Delhi, where he had taken a house in Shahdara. We were there hardly for six or seven days, trying to bring order to our thoughts and our home, when the river Yamuna went into spate—bursting its banks at 5 p.m., and by 6–7 p.m. the whole ground floor of our home was flooded.

My father took two coir-matted *charpoys*, tied them together and then tied all three of us to the charpoy, using it as a float. He bade us goodbye, saying 'Where there is life, there is hope, and if God so wills, we will meet again', and set us adrift in the swirling waters. We were crying and screaming but the charpoy went on its merry way till it hit the railway tracks on the other side and snagged.

Fortune favoured us and a steam engine rolled by. The driver saw us and heard our frightened screams. He stopped the train and, through what I think was Morse code, contacted the stationmaster, who instructed him to bring us to the station and give us dry clothes and food. We were there for two days with no news of our parents.

Meanwhile, our parents spent the night on the terrace back home. In the morning, my mother felt the house shaking and suggested to my father to move down to the rooms on the periphery, so that when the house collapsed, they will not be buried under the debris. In the early hours my father's partner hired an elephant to pull them out of the house and the flood. But the mahout was a Muslim, and refused to help a Hindu in distress. And yet he lived in India and called himself an Indian, but then India is a secular state!

In the morning, the floodwaters started receding and help came in the form of volunteers with thick ropes to rescue those who were stranded. Now came the most difficult task of finding us. We were given balcony space at the stationmaster's house in Ghaziabad and told to fend for ourselves as the stationmaster was not supposed to house us.

Announcements were made every day for separated families and we were united with our parents after three months.

The stationmaster was a kind man but he said he would lose his job if he housed so many people in his quarters. He got a coolie to clean out a four-foot by ten-foot room in the porter's quarters and gave it to our family of five, where we cooked, cleaned ourselves up and slept.

All the gold jewellery was sold piecemeal for sustenance. Studies went for a toss. The boys would stand in line for one aluminium mug or a jug or a blanket or whatever the philanthropists distributed. They would wait on railway tracks for hours till an engine passed by, leaving in its wake a trail of burnt out coal called coke, which they would bring back home for Mother to use in cooking. No coke, no meal.

Wherever we went, we went together for fear of being separated.

Money was needed for survival, and my father thought we had taken enough advantage of the stationmaster's hospitality. Bombay was a better place for business and so we moved to a Bombay camp. My father, once a businessman, became a door-to-door salesman! He started selling batteries, and on one of his rounds, landed at Mohammed Ali Road. At the corner was a crockery shop—Bellaram's. He walked in to sell his wares and saw a familiar face. Mr Tulli!

He recognized Father immediately. Mr Tulli asked if he was looking for a job, then the former could ask his boss to give one to Father right then. So, Father became a showroom salesman. We were all so happy that instead of roaming in the sun and rain he would have a sheltered workplace and earn a steady income, however meagre.

After a few days, he met Mr Krishanchand Khanna—actor Vinod Khanna's father—who, by way of conversation, came to know of our family's plight. He offered us rooms in a small place, a chawl, at Kandivli. It felt like heaven. We moved to our new home with a few possessions and started to put together our scattered life.

We enrolled at Sheth N.L. Hindi High School. My elder bother passed his Metric (school-leaving) examination and got a job with Hindustan Petroleum, with living quarters to boot. The family moved again, but now to a permanent home at Chembur. I graduated from school and got admission in R.A. Podar College. I used to cycle to college every day so as to save the conveyance fare. Good exercise! I graduated and joined Mahindra's as a clerk in the accounts department and retired as their accounts manager.

I applied for a flat in the upcoming M.G. Colony and was allotted a home by lottery.

Prabha's elder sister's husband was my friend. I met Prabha, married her and every sorrow is behind us now. We can truly say, 'And they lived happily ever after...'

23 Nimoo Sadarangani

I was born Nirmala Hiranand Uttamsing in the year 1936 in Hyderabad, Sindh. The Gandhian movement started in 1942 and we became aware of the Quit India movement.

Soon afterwards we heard that British rule in India was coming to an end and that Hindus and Muslims will be separated. As children, we were in a happy frame of mind. Little did we realize that great was going to be the fall of the country and the British were not going to give up such a prized colony so easily.

At the beginning of the year 1947, trouble had been brewing in the Punjab province. My father, who was a history teacher at Kundanmal Girls' High School (where most of the Amil community sent their girls), sensed the unrest. He had friends in high places and, after much consultation, thought it wiser to camp out across the border for some time, and made arrangements accordingly. He was advised to take as little luggage as possible, maybe to show the outsiders that we were just going for a holiday.

I had two sisters, an older one named Maina and a younger one, Shirley. Our mother made us wear dress upon dress to minimize the luggage, tied the family cash, jewellery and documents around our waists, locked the house and we headed to the station. My father was accompanied by his unmarried sister Totibai, his young, widowed sister Gopibai, her two children, her brother-in-law Mr Gobindram Ramchandani, who was a retired forest officer, and his three children.

We crossed the border and reached Nadiad on the Indian side, where arrangements had been made for us at an ashram. It was a huge hall with plenty of space for all to be comfortable, except that the toilets were far away. As was the custom then, the toilets were built in the furthermost corner of the compound as there were no septic tanks in those days, only open drainage. Not being used to it, we would go out in groups after sundown.

While at Nadiad, we heard about the division of the country into Hindustan and Pakistan and realized that we will never see our native land again. We also understood why we had to wear dress upon dress and take as much treasure as we could on us, as the house we locked up merely became a key in our possession.

Now came the question of resettlement and the beginning of a new life. My father applied for a job at Gujarat University and was appointed Professor of History at Ahmedabad College. Seeing the circumstances, he got living quarters on the campus and moved his family from Nadiad to Ahmedabad. We were enrolled at the Sindh Academy School. My aunt Gopi's family, the Ramchandanis, went off to Bombay, where they had some relatives.

We stayed on in Ahmedabad till my father passed away in 1953. We were devastated. My aunts Gopibai and Totibai entreated us to pack our bags and come to Bombay. We managed to get paying guest accommodation at Shyam Nivas, a new colony on Warden Road, which housed most of the Amil community. Maina and I started working while studying. Shirley went to school and helped Mother with household chores.

Maina and I took classes in typing and shorthand, as secretarial jobs were easier to find on a part-time basis and the family income had to be augmented. Diligent and honest work paid off and from there the graph could only go up.

At the border crossing, one incident comes to mind. Muslims who were going in the opposite direction, mostly villagers, asked Aunt Toti, '*Aap ka jharoo kaisa hua?*' Being a typical Sindhi and having no inkling of Hindi, she did not understand that these people meant, 'How was the search conducted at the border?'

She told them, there was no jharoo, only *buhwari*, the Sindhi word for jharoo, meaning broom. What a laugh it was!

24 Ratna Mukhi

Talks about the division of India had started and there was trouble between Hindus and Muslims. My elder brother, Kishin, had a sixth sense that all did not bode well. In 1946, he told our parents to leave Hyderabad before the trouble began and they got caught in the crossfire.

Stories came from Punjab that girls were being abducted. As it is the illiterate Muslim population from the Sindhi villages had their eyes on the towns and cities of Sindh. Sindhi girls were considered beauties by them—fairies or hoors, angels from paradise.

Our parents decided to take Kishin's advice, leave the land of their birth, and move to a safer haven. But why Bombay? It was a city of opportunities—good businesses, good schools and colleges, world-recognized universities and the elite of the community stayed there. Many holidays had been spent there and it was familiar ground.

One brother was already married, and a sister got married as Partition closed in. The year was 1947 but we were prepared for the move. My brother had sold several bungalows, our immovable properties, for which he got a good price. I was 10 years old at the time and Bombay was like the America of today—across the seven seas.

The family took a flight to Bombay, booked four rooms at the Sea Green Hotel and we stayed there for two months. We had the wherewithal, having liquidated all our properties, and had hard cash with us. At the end of two months the hotel bill amounted to Rs 22,000, a princely sum at that time when everything was at sixes and sevens. My father bade Kishin get a spacious apartment for the family. He found one close by, at Prem Court near KC College. Very central. Close to the business district and educational institutes.

The rent was negligible but he had to pay *pugree*, or money on goodwill, of Rs 18,000. It was the right time to have moved because from then on housing choices quickly became scarce and pugree rates increased.

As refugees started pouring in, the city seemed to burst at the seams. Conditions became increasingly difficult. Refugee camps were set up to accomodate the multitude. *Lakhpatis* became *kakhpatis* overnight.

We thanked the Lord—and my brother—for the timely move. Generations have since lived in this house—Prem Court. The grandchildren still reside there with their families and have seen no hard times.

25 Kala

I was born Pushpa Belaram Chhabria but after marriage became Kala Dhiraj Mahajan. In my time, one could not question their parents in the choice of a marriage partner. I belonged to a rich family, which owned a sweetmeat store in Jacobabad. It was very famous for its authentic sweets, and anybody who was somebody shopped there. My father's family were also landowners, like most Sindhis. My uncles owned rice mills. We lived happily in a joint family.

Life dealt me its first cruel blow when I was married off to an alcoholic and had three daughters in succession. They were very pretty girls and so dear to me, but my husband could not look after us and spent all he earned on alcohol. In the end he abandoned us, just as Partition set in, in 1947.

There were plenty of Muslims in Jacobabad and I was afraid for my girls. The Muslims would taunt us, and throw mud on our clean outfits, so I and part of the family decided to leave. My uncles went to Hyderabad to get train tickets for us but returned empty-handed.

In their absence, conditions in Jacobabad became intolerable. We could not send the children to school, nor had we any answers to the many questions they asked. Trains coming into the city were overloaded with refugees, who did not hesitate to loot or kill. We saw children, including babies, being nailed to walls and fences and young girls kidnapped and raped. It was like going back in time to the rule of Kamsa, who killed his own sister's babies by dashing them against walls.

My uncles were determined to send us across the border. So they went to Hyderabad with the whole family in tow—about 20 of us. This time we got the tickets but only a coupe to accommodate all of us. Each person was allowed to take only four dresses and as much jewellery and documents as we could carry on us.

Most of my gold jewellery I sold, not knowing what the future held for us, and hard cash was a prime factor. My jewellery was sold for Rs 30 a tola or 11.5 gm in Indian measure. Even at that time it would have fetched Rs 300 for 10 gm, but beggars cannot be choosers and we took what we got. The migration took place in the dead of night. No one uttered a word for fear of being heard. People who could not get tickets took a chance and travelled on the roof of the train.

I saw my aunt being hit on the head, but there was nothing to do except go forward as if she was not one of us. We hid till the goons disappeared, then quickly carried her to the train and gave her first aid. After reaching the station of Chhor, we were able to talk in whispers and headed further to Udaipur and safety.

A family travelling on the same train lost their mother who probably could not bear the shock of leaving her hearth and home for unknown places. Her children could not pick up the corpse and take it with them nor could they stay back to perform her last rites as they were unsure of their own future. They saw the body being trampled over but boarded the train, grieving for the mother they had lost.

All of us left the comfort of our homes in an as-is-where-is condition. The very domestics who assured us safety took our homes and businesses as if it was theirs and we could do nothing about it but thank them for being kind to us!

Our guru, Dada Sai, came to our aid. Mata Hari and Sai, through some refugee officers, got Haji Pir Gardens and the rooms therein vacated. Each family was allotted one room. We stayed there for one year. With Sai's help and blessings, we moved to Bombay—as the streets of Bombay were paved with gold—and got a room at Chowpatty, near National Garage, for which we paid a monthly rent of Rs 400.

I started making papads and sold them, mostly to Sindhis. I became known. My papads grew so popular that other communities started buying them. I also took up embroidery work—saris, dresses, linen—and was paid well for my work. Thus, my girls were able to go to school and finish their interrupted education.

I don't know how my husband found us. Thinking he had turned over a new leaf, I took him back into the fold. But a leopard never changes its spots. After I gave birth to two boys, my husband Dhiraj just disappeared. Now it became a struggle to rear five children instead of three!

Guruji's blessings were upon us, and we moved to a bigger house at Walkeshwar for a pugree—an illegal possession and deal for the house. We lived here for 10–12 years. By then, the children grew up and were able to help in every way.

Sai's relatives, Duru and Sundari, qualified as doctors and started the Mata Hari Laxmi Hospital in their mother's name and did yeoman service. They helped everyone who went to them.

One of Dada Sai's disciples met me at a religious gathering and out of the kindness of her heart suggested I move to a better locality for the sake of my children, who were now of marriageable age. She said she had invested in a building on Altamount Road called Navjivan Apartments. It was ready for possession and if I so desired, she would sell it to me for Rs 22,000, the original price, and take no profit on it.

It was a wonderful offer! I went home and consulted with the children. Enquiries were also made for a settlement with our landlord, who wanted a Rs 10,000 premium to transfer the house to me. A deal was struck. Being in my name it was easy to sell the flat. I got Rs 36,000 for it from which I paid off all dues and the Altamount Road flat became my very own property.

Today my daughters and sons are married into well-to-do families and are well settled and lead a good life. My youngest daughter, Shyama, chose not to marry. She lives with me and has a successful tailoring house and does catering of chocolates, sweetmeats, etc.

You name it, she does it. I suppose she has inherited my genes.

Aaya Pir, Bhagga Mir and Other Sindhi Proverbs

Sarla Nari Kripalani

Foreword by
Dada J. P. Vaswani

Foreword

Proverbs and sayings are not merely pleasant or interesting words strung together. They encapsulate within them the essence of a community's beliefs, teachings, language, wisdom and culture.

A proverb, to be worthy of the name, need not be clever, but should be satisfying. For instance, 'Lend your money and lose your friend' is a great proverb, familiar in almost every language. A great proverb instructs without preaching. Though astringent, it is never bitter. A proverb conveys its message in the fewest possible words: it may tease, but it neither stings nor leaves an unpleasant aftertaste. It summarizes a situation in a nutshell, drives home the point and often appeals to our sense of humour.

Mrs Sarla Nari Kripalani is a woman with a rich mind, a beautiful heart and radiant simplicity. She is a person of knowledge, understanding, love. Her life is a mine of many virtues. She has taken great care to collect a number of Sindhi proverbs and provide their equivalents in the English language. How true it is that proverbial wisdom is wholly international.

These pithy, concise and concentrated sayings offer insight into the depth, mindset and perceptions of our Sindhi ancestors, making us privy to their common sense, knowledge, experience and wisdom.

This little book, if utilized thoughtfully, can serve as a measuring stick for assessing different situations and making wise decisions when dealing with them.

—J.P. Vaswani
Pune, March 2008

Preface

Every language has been enriched by proverbs rooted in the ethos and traditions of the particular community to which the language belongs. The Sindhi language is earthy, vibrant and lucid. It encompasses many proverbs that reflect the cultural moorings of the community. Sindhi literature, which is rich and descriptive in itself, is made even more colourful by the use of proverbs. Of course, over the years, some proverbs have been added, while others have faded away. As society evolves and changes, so do its proverbs. Sindhi society has seen many shifts in its history. It has experienced both the superimposition of Islamic culture and the Arabic language, and the trauma of disconnection from the land of its birth following Partition, resulting in its immersion into a multilingual environment in post-Partition India. While the Arabic script was adopted for formal use in the Sindhi language, Sindhi identity remained intact in its land of origin. However, in post-Partition India, Sindhi speakers were relocated into regions where several other languages predominated. Consequently, the Sindhi language now struggles desperately to maintain its distinct identity.

It is the proverbs that have come to the rescue in spoken Sindhi, as the older generation continues to use them with the younger generation in order to drive home a point. The younger generation may not fully understand or speak the language in its purest form, but they certainly understand the proverbs.

Until now, no one had thought of compiling these proverbs into a document of archival value. This daunting and stupendous task has been undertaken by the graceful Sarla Kripalani, who has done so with great love and dedication. Sarla possesses a wealth of knowledge as far as the Sindhi language is concerned. She has meticulously translated the proverbs into English for the benefit of future generations. The Sindhi language has weathered many storms, but as long as there are dedicated and selfless people like Sarla nurturing it, we have nothing to fear. Sarla has created a unique legacy, and the Sindhi community salutes her for her devotion and sincerity.

—**Dr (Ms) Subhadra Anand**
Principal (Retd), R.D. National College
Author of *National Integration of Sindhis*
Mumbai, April 2008

Introduction

You must wonder why I chose *Aaya Pir, Bhagga Mir*—the clergy came, and the feudal aristocracy fled—as the title of this book. It seemed the most appropriate, given the events. India had its maharajas, and Sindh (now in Pakistan) had its mirs. The Mirs, or Sindhi aristocracy, were feudal lords who lived lavishly, with wine, women and song. Sindh—the cradle of the Indus Valley civilization—was fertile and enriched them greatly. They led a decadent life while the pirs, the religious class, observed the deterioration of Sindh's society.

The British, to serve their own interests, dismantled the Mir dynasty. This created an opportunity for the clergy, the pirs, to step in. At the turn of the century, the pirs took Sindh by storm and established a new religious order. They amassed a large following and became extremely powerful, seeking to influence the younger generation, whom they saw drifting away from religion and discipline. Sindh changed, its culture changed, its rulers changed. The religious class of pirs and mullahs became the de facto rulers of Pakistan. Their word became law and still is, as evidenced by the prevailing conditions in that country. Therefore, the proverb remains topical.

Even though our national anthem includes Sindh along with other provinces, Sindhis, alone, of all Indians, have no state they can call their own. Yet, they are a proud people who, through dint of hard work, have integrated themselves across every state in India—nay, the whole world—and have risen to great heights as educationists, industrialists, philanthropists, professionals and politicians. Partition taught us many lessons. To preserve our culture was the foremost. Retaining the language, however, was not always possible, as children had to learn the national language and the state language, as also the language of the world, i.e. English. Thus, Sindhi had to be shelved.

Like my mother, there were many others who did not let their children forget the language entirely. My parents were still in Karachi at the time of Partition, while I had been sent to India. My mother, even though she knew English, insisted on writing to me in Sindhi. Of course, I would invariably reply in English. Her contention was that if you have a mother-in-law who knows no English, how will you communicate? I told her I'll marry an Englishman, and that will solve all problems!

Right from my childhood I had been hearing *pahakaas* or proverbs, from my mother and grandmother and, after I got married, from my mother-in-law. As they were getting old, it struck me that such a beautiful pahakaa culture might be lost forever. That is how I started writing them down and understanding their meanings. A simple proverb like '*Andhan Multan ladho*' was often repeated. If I asked, 'Mummy and Ami, where in Colaba can I find this address?' they would reply: 'Andhan Multan ladho and you can't locate this place?'

Evidently, the road from Hyderabad, Sindh, to Multan was so straight that even a blind man could follow it unaided. '*Ditho pir puni murad*'—you may long for something, but the moment you attain it, you lose interest. '*Piya sandas pehoon kutyoon daday sandas dhauran agay puchhandahua zaat and paat, hearan puchhan thha naran*'—in the good old days, ancestry took precedence over all else; it didn't matter if you had to do manual work to earn a living, as long as your lineage was honourable. Marriages were unions of families, not just the bride and groom. Today, it's wealth that counts. A fat bank balance, even if ill-gotten, is enough to satisfy everyone.

The proverbs are a rich heritage of my beloved Sindh, my native land. Many listed in this book are unique to Sindhi culture and have no equivalent in other languages. I have still tried to find English equivalents to help younger generations connect with their linguistic heritage. But some proverbs are untranslatable. Sindhi, with its 52 letters and rich phonetics, is truly a unique language.

The book appears in three scripts and languages: Sindhi, Hindi, English. The English provides the equivalent proverb to the Sindhi, illustrating the universality of proverbial wisdom. The Devanagari script renders the Sindhi into Hindi, and the Roman script aids in pronunciation.

Late Mrs Guli Gobindram Bhavnani

I began this collection in 1980. I realized that my two mothers—my mother and, later, my mother-in-law—used proverbs freely in conversation, and so aptly! As they approached old age, I feared the treasure of the Sindhi language would die with them. I started compiling these proverbs as a hobby. It soon became a passion, and now, an obsession. I scribble on paper napkins, bills, visiting cards, any blank piece of paper I can find, whenever I hear something new or recall a proverb from distant memory. Now, there's no stopping. My mothers, Mrs Guli Gobindram Bhavnani and Mrs Sarasati Manghanmal Kripalani, have since departed for their heavenly abode, but the enthusiasm continues. I dedicate this work to their memory.

A few quotes on the significance of proverbs in daily life: 'The storehouse of wisdom is stocked with proverbs,' goes an ancient Persian saying. 'A proverb is a short sentence based on a long experience,' said Miguel de Cervantes, author of *Don Quixote*. 'Proverbs,' noted Ralph Waldo Emerson, the great American poet, 'are the sanctuary of the intuitions.' 'A proverb

Late Mrs Sarasati Manghanmal Kripalani

is anonymous human history compressed to the size of a seed,' according to Stephan Käufer in *Proverbs & Aphorisms*. Hamlet, the Prince of Denmark, however, had no patience for proverbs. 'The proverb is something musty,' he said disdainfully. 'Yet William Shakespeare's plays overflow with "musty somethings",' says Käufer. Like, 'Men are April when they woo and December when they wed'; 'A little pot and soon hot'; 'The fashion wears out more apparel than the man'; or, for Hamlet's use, 'Patch grief with proverbs'.

Proverbs and aphorisms were highly popular with the British by the mid-nineteenth century, but they've been used for centuries across the world. Some of the proverbs in this book date as far back as the 1600s. How did they originate? I would say they are the collective wisdom of our elders, used to gently guide the younger generation. It's not for nothing that 'grey hairs are the blooms of experience' or *'vaar uss mein kann accha thiya ahin'* as it is said in Sindhi:

وار اُس ۾ ڪان اڇا ٿيا آهن

There are about 3,000 Sindhi proverbs. Many of them were brought by migrants who came to 'Scinde' from Punjab, Rajasthan, Gujarat, Multan and Afghanistan. Hence, they are not purely Sindhi in origin, but bear a blend of influences. This book, with its two hundred or so proverbs, is a modest attempt to preserve and record the oft-repeated proverbs of the Sindhi language.

—Sarla Nari Kripalani
Mumbai, July 2008

Sindhi Proverbs and Their English Equivalents

كائيندي كُوهه
به كُتي وَجن

Khaaeende khooh[a] bi khutee vanyan[i]

खाईंदे खूह बि खुटी वजनि

Always taking out and never putting back, soon empties the biggest sack.

كائيندي	khaaeende	खाईंदे	to consume
كوهه	khooh[a]	खूह	wells
كُتي	khutee	खुटी	empty

بچَت آهي اُپت

Bachat[i] aahe upat[i]

बचति आहे उपति

A penny saved is a penny earned.

| بچَت | bachat[i] | बचति | saving |
| اُپت | upat[i] | उपति | earning |

رِيوُن مِڙيوئي
بوُٽ ڪاريون

Ridhoo[n] midyoee booth[a] kaar[i]yoo[n]

रिढूं मिड़ियोई बूथ कारियूं

All cats are grey in the dark.

رِيوُن	ridhoo[n]	रिढूं	lambs
بوُٽ	booth[a]	बूथ	snout
ڪاريون	kaariyoo[n]	कारियूं	black

جھڙو سنگُ،
تھڙو رنگُ

Jeh[i]do sang[u], teh[i]do rang[u]

जहिड़ो संगु तहिड़ो रंगु

A man is known by the company he keeps.

| سنگُ | sang[u] | संगु | company |
| رنگُ | rang[u] | रंगु | habit |

اَدّ کي چِڍي
سڄي ڍانھن
ڊوڙجي، ته اَدُ
بہ وِڃائجي

Adh[a] khe chha_d_e, saje _d_aa[n]h[un] dodje, ta adh[u] bi vinyaaije

अध खे छड़े सज़े ड़ांहु डोड़िजे, त अधु बि विञाइजे

A bird in hand is worth two in the bush.

اَدّ	adh[a]	अध्	half
چڍي	chha_d_e	छड़े	leave
سڄي	saje	सज़े	whole
وِڃائجي	vinyaaije	विञाइजे	lose

ٽٽُونءَ کي
ٽارو، تازيءَ
کي اِشارو

Tatoo[n-a] khe taaro, taazee[a] khe ishaaro

टटूंअ खे टारो, ताज़ीअ खे इशारो

A nod for the wise man and a rod for the fool.

ٽٽُون	tatoo[n-a]	टटूं	slowpoke mule
ٽارو	taaro	टारो	whip
تازي	taazee[a]	ताज़ी	fine steed
اِشارو	ishaaro	इशारो	spur

جھڙي پوکبي،
تھڙي لڻبي

Jeh[i]dee pokh[i]bee, teh[i]dee lun[i]bee

जहिड़ी पोखिबी, तहिड़ी लुणिबी

As you sow, so shall you reap.

| پوکبي | pokh[i]bee | पोखिबी | sow |
| لڻبي | lun[i]bee | लुणिबी | reap |

کیر جو کانیلُ،
جهَڻِ بہ ڦُوڪي
پیئي

Kheer[a] jo khaa[n]yal[u], jhan[i] bi phooke peeye
खीर जो खांयलु, झणि बि फूके पीये
Once burnt, twice shy.

کیر	kheer[a]	खीर	milk
کا نیلُ	khaa[n]yal[u]	खांयलु	burnt
جهَڻِ	jhan[i]	झणि	buttermilk
ڦُوڪي	phooke	फूके	blow on to cool

دوست اُهو جو
یار غار رهي

Dost[u] uho jo yaar gaar[u] rahe
दोस्तु उहो जो यार ग़ारु रहे
A friend in need is a friend indeed.

| دوست | dost[u] | दोस्तु | friend |
| یار غارُ | yaar gaar[u] | यार ग़ारु | help-in-need |

هر هلڪائي نہ
وڃ، در دوستن
جي

Har[i] halkaaee na vany[u], dar[i] dostan[i] je
हरि हलकाई न वञु, दरि दोस्तनि जे
A constant guest is never welcome.

هلڪائي	halkaaee	हलकाई	lightly
در	dar[i]	दर	door
دوستن	dostan[i]	दोस्तनि	friends

پڙهي پاڻ نہ
ڄاڻي، ماري
ڪتابي

Padhee paan[a] na jaane, maare kitaabee
पढ़ी पाण न जाणे, मारे किताबी
A bad workman blames his tools.

پڙهي	padhee	पढ़ी	read
ڪتابي	kitaabee	किताबी	student
ڄاڻي	jaane	जाणे	to know
ماري	maare	मारे	hits

Aaya Pir, Bhagga Mir and Other Sindhi Proverbs

بابو آچاري، پَرَ کو مَڃي

Baabo aachaaree, par^a ko manye

बाबो आचारी, पर को मञे

A prophet is not without honour save in his own country.

بابو	baabo	बाबो	father, elder
آچاري	aachaaree	आचारी	teacher
مڃي	manye	मञे	acknowledge

گهَرَ جو پِيرُ، چُلهِه جو مارنگ

Ghar^a jo peer^u, chulhⁱ jo maarang^u

घर जो पीरु, चुल्हि जो मारंगु

A saint is not recognized in his own country.

گهَرَ	ghar^a	घर	home
پِيرُ	peer^u	पीरु	family patriarch
چُلهِه	chulhⁱ	चुल्हि	hearth
مارنگ	maarang^u	मारंगु	temporary hearth made from a few stones

اُٺ جي وات ۾ جِيرو

Uth^a je vaat^a meiⁿ jeero

उठ जे वात् में जीरो

A drop in the ocean.

اُٺ	uth^a	उठ	camel
وات	vaat^a	वात	mouth
جِيرو	jeero	जीरो	cumin seed

جِڀَ جي
تِرڪَڻَ کاءُ،
پيرَ جو تِرڪَڻُ چڱو

Jibh[a] je tirkan[a] khaa[n], per[a] jo tirkan[u] chango

ज़िभ जे तिरकण खां, पेर जो तिरकणु चङो

A slip of the foot you may soon recover, but a slip of the tongue you may never get over.

ڄڀ	jibh[a]	ज़िभ	tongue
ترڪڻ	tirkan[a]	तिरकण	slip
پير	per[a]	पेर	foot
چڱو	chango	चङो	better

آهي ته عيد، نَه
ته روزو

Aahe ta eed[a], na ta rozo

आहे त ईद, न त रोज़ो

Always a feast or a famine.

عيد	eed[a]	ईद	Eid
نَه ته	na ta	न त	or else
روزو	rozo	रोज़ो	fast

سهسين ڪري
سينگار،
ڪوڏڙيءَ پُٽُ
ڪوڏڙو

Sahise[n] kare seengaar[a], khodidee[a] put[u] khodido

सहिसें करे सींगार, खोदिड़ीअ पुटु खोदिड़ो

An ass is but an ass, though laden with gold.

سهسين	sahise[n]	सहिसें	hundred times
سينگار	seengaar[a]	सींगार	adorn
ڪوڏڙي	khodido	ख़ोदड़ी	ass
پُٽ	put[u]	पुटु	son

گَدَهَ چا جاڻنِ
گیهَرَن مان

Ga<u>d</u>ah[a] chhaa jaanan[i] geeharan[i] maa[n]

गड़ह छा जाणनि गीहरनि मां

What will asses know of the value of fine food.

گَدَهَ	ga<u>d</u>ah[a]	गड़ह	ass
جاڻنِ	jaanan[i]	जाणनि	know
گیهَر	geehar	गीहर	jalebi

آرسِيءَ جو ڏارُ
ءِ دل جو ڏارُ،
سالِمُ نه ٿئي

Aarsee[a] jo <u>d</u>aar[u] ai[n] dil[i] jo <u>d</u>aar[u] saalim[u] na thiye

आर्सी[अ] जो ड़ारु ऐं दिलि जो ड़ारु, सालिमु न थिए

A cracked mirror and a broken heart cannot be mended with silk.

آرسي	aarsee[a]	आर्सी	mirror
ڏار	<u>d</u>aar[u]	ड़ार	crack
سالم	saalim[u]	सालिमु	mended

جِيءُ خوشِ ته
جهانُ خوش

Jee[u] khush[i] ta jahaan[u] khush

जीउ खुशि त जहानु खुशि

Health is wealth.

جِيءُ	jee[u]	जीउ	health, body
خوشِ	khush[i]	खुशि	happy
جهانُ	jahaan[u]	जहानु	world

باهِراں زيب زَبان، دِلِ مِ هچارو

Baahiraaⁿ zeb^i zabaan, dil^i meiⁿ hachaaro

बाहिरां ज़ेब ज़बान, दिलि में हचारो

A cross on the breast, the devil in the heart.

باهران	Baahiraaⁿ	बाहिरां	outer
زيب زبان	zeb^i zabaan	ज़ेब ज़बान	sweet tongue
دِلِ	dil^i	दिलि	heart
هچارو	hachaaro	हचारो	murderer

پُٽُ ٿئي مال ڀائي، ڌيءَ ٿئي حال ڀائي

Put^u thiye maal^a bhaae^e, dhee^a thiye haal^a bhaae^e

पुटु थिए माल भाई, धीअ थिए हाल भाई

A son is a son till he gets himself a wife, a daughter is a daughter all her life.

پُٽ	put^u	पुट	son
مال ڀائي	maal^a bhaae^e	माल भाई	business partner
ڌيءَ	dhee^a	धीअ	daughter
حال ڀائي	haal^a bhaae^e	हाल भाई	health partner

ٿوري کٽڻي گهڻي برڪت

Thore khatie, ghanee barkat^a

थोरे खटिए, घणी बरकत

Low margins, high profits.

ٿوري	thore	थोरे	less
کٽڻي	khatie	खटिए	profit
گهڻي	ghanee	घणी	more
برڪت	barkat^a	बरकत	fulfilment

Aaya Pir, Bhagga Mir and Other Sindhi Proverbs • 107

جھڑا کانگ،
تھڑا بچڑا

Jeh[i]daa kaang[a], teh[i]daa bach[i]daa

जहिड़ा कांग, तहिड़ा बचिड़ा

As the old bird sings, so will the young ones twitter.

| کانگ | kaang[a] | कांग | crows |
| بچڑا | bach[i]daa | बचिड़ा | babies |

اِهائي زبان
عرش تي
پهُچائي، اِهائي
زبان فرش تي

Ihaaee zabaan arsh[a] te pahuchaae, ihaaee zabaan farsh[a] te

इहाई ज़बान अर्श ते पहुचाए, इहाई ज़बान फ़र्श ते

A bridle for the tongue is a necessary piece of furniture.

زبان	zabaan	ज़बान	tongue
عرش	arsh[a]	अर्श	sky
پهچائي	pahuchaae	पहुचाए	reach
فرش	farsh[a]	फ़र्श	carpet

سکڻي کُني
گهڻو اُڀامي

Sakh[i]nee kunee ghano ubhaame

सखिणी कुनी घणो उभामे

A little pot and soon hot.

سکڻي	sakh[i]nee	सखिणी	empty
کُني	kunee	कुनी	pot
گهڻو	ghano	घणो	more
اُڀامي	ubhaame	उभामे	boil over

نَئِين ڪنوار نَوَ
ڏِينهن، لَٿي پَٿي
ڏَهَ ڏِينهن

Naeeⁿ kuⁿwaarⁱ nav^a deenh^{an}, lathe pathe dah^a deenh^{an}

नई कुंआरि नव ड़ींह, लथे पथे ड़ह ड़ींह

A new broom is good for three days.

ڪنوارِ	kuⁿwaarⁱ	कुंआरि	bride
نَوَ	nav^a	नव	nine
لَٿي پَٿي	lathe pathe	लथे पथे	at most
ڏَهَ	dah^a	ड़ह	ten
ڏِينهن	deeⁿh^{an}	ड़ींह	days

ٻوڙو کِلي ٻه دفعا

Bodo khile ba dafaa

बोड़ो खिले ब दफ़ा

A deaf fool laughs when others laugh.

ٻوڙو	bodo	बोड़ो	deaf
کِلي	khile	खिले	laughs
ٻه دفعا	ba dafaa	ब दफ़ा	twice

آڻِ مڃي، جھڳڙا ٽوٽا

Aanⁱ manyee, jhagⁱdaa toota

आणि मञी, झगिड़ा टूटा

A fault confessed is half redressed.

آڻِ مڃي	aanⁱ manyee	आणि मञी	accept defeat
جھڳڙا	jhagⁱdaa	झगिड़ा	fight
ٽوٽا	toota	टूटा	settled

Aaya Pir, Bhagga Mir and Other Sindhi Proverbs

Chintaa aisee daakⁱnee, kaatⁱ kalejaa khaay, vaid bechaaraa kya kare, kab tak marham lagaay

चिंता ऐसी डाकिनी, काटि कलेजा खाय, वैद बेचारा क्या करे, कब तक मरहम लगाय

As rust eats iron, so care eats the heart.

چِنتا	chintaa	चिंता	worry
داڪِني	dakⁱnee	डाकिनी	witch
ڪَليجا	kalejaa	कलेजा	liver
ڪاءِ	khaay	खाय	eats
وِند	vaid	वैद	doctor
مرهم	marham	मरहम	balm

Jo gasⁱyo, so vasⁱyo

जो गसियो, सो वसियो

The used key shines the brightest.

گسِيو	gasⁱyo	गसियो	used
وسِيو	vasⁱyo	वसियो	success

Jo saje jee khwaahishᵃ kare, uho adhᵘ bi vinyaaee

जो सजे जी ख़्वाहिश करे, उहो अधु बि विञाए

All covet, all lose.

خواهش	khwaahishᵃ	ख़्वाहिश	desire
وِڃائي	vinyaaee	विञाए	lose

سچو سائینءَ
جو سباجهو

Sacho Saaee[n-a] jo sabaajho

सचो साईं[अ] जो सबाझो

An honest man is the noblest work of God.

سچو	sacho	सचो	honest
سائینءَ جو	saaee[n-a] jo	साईं[अ] जो	God's
سباجهو	sabaajho	सबाझो	blessed

سَوَ ڏينهن
چور جا، هِكُ
ڏينهن ساڌَ جو

Sau dee[n]h[an] chor[a] jaa, hik[u] dee[n]h[un] saadh[a] jo

सौ डींहं चोर जा, हिकु डींहुं साध जो

An honest man scares thirty thieves.

سَوَ	sau	सौ	hundred
ڏينهن	dee[n]h[an]	डींहं	days
چور	chor[a]	चोर	thief
هِكُ	hik[u]	हिकु	one
ساڌَ	saadh[a]	साध	saint

اُماس ۽ چاندني
بَئي ڀينرون

Umaas[a] ai[n] chaand[a]nee baee bhen[a]roo[n]

उमास ऐं चांदनी बई भेनरूं

After dusk comes dawn.

اُماس	umaas[a]	उमास	moonless night
چاندني	chaand[a]nee	चांदनी	moonlight
ڀينرون	bhen[a]roo[n]	भेनरूं	sisters

صُبُح جو صَرفو، سَجي ڏينهن جي بَچَتِ

Subuh[a] jo sarfo, saje deenhan jee bachat[i]

सुबुह जो सफ़ो, सजे ड़ींह जी बचति

A bit in the morning is better than nothing all day.

صُبُح	subuh[a]	सुबुह	morning
صَرفو	sarfo	सफ़ो	income
سَجي ڏينهن	saje deenhan	सजे ड़ींह	all day
بَچَتِ	bachat[i]	बचति	saving

پيار ۽ جنگ ۾ سڀُ جائز

Pyaar[a] ai[n] jang[i] mei[n] sabh[u] jaaiz

प्यार ऐं जंगि में सभु जाइज़

All is fair in love and war.

پيار	pyaar[a]	प्यार	love
جنگ	jang[i]	जंगि	war
جائز	jaaiz	जाइज	fair

جهڙي ڪرڻي، تهڙي ڀرڻي، جهڙي نيت، تهڙي مُراد

Jeh[i]dee kar[i]nee, teh[i]dee bhar[i]nee, jeh[i]dee niyat[a], teh[i]dee muraad[a]

जहिड़ी करिणी, तहिड़ी भरिणी, जहिड़ी नियत, तहिड़ी मुराद

An eye for an eye and a tooth for a tooth.

جهڙي	jeh[i]dee	जहिड़ी	as
ڪرڻي	kar[i]nee	करिणी	deed
نيت	niyat[a]	नियत	intention
مُراد	muraad[a]	मुराद	desire

هِڪَ گهَڙِيءَ
جي خطا،
صدِيُنِ جي سزا

Hik^a ghadee^a jee khataa, sadiyunⁱ jee sazaa

हिक घड़ी^अ जी ख़ता, सदियुनि जी सज़ा

Anger and haste hinder good counsel.

هِڪَ	hik^a	हिक	one
گهَڙِي	ghadee^a	घड़ी	moment
خطا	khataa	ख़ता	error
صدِيُنِ	sadiyunⁱ	सदियुनि	centuries
سزا	sazaa	सज़ा	penalty

قَنِ مَتان لوُنُ
چِٽَڪَڻُ

Phatanⁱ mathaaⁿ loon^u chhanⁱkan^u

फटनि मथां लूणु छणिकणु

Adding salt to wounds.

قَنِ	phatanⁱ	फटनि	wounds
مَتان	mathaaⁿ	मथां	on
لوُنُ	loon^u	लूणु	salt
چِٽَڪَڻُ	chhanⁱkan^u	छणिकणु	sprinkle

سَڀِڪو پنھنجي
هَٽِيءَ جو
هوڪو ڏِني

Sabhⁱko peⁿhinjee^a hatee^a jo hoko <u>d</u>iye

सभिको पंहिंजी हटी^अ जो होको ड़िए

Blow your own trumpet.

هَٽِي	hatee^a	हटी	shop
هوڪو	hoko	होको	hawker's cry

Aaya Pir, Bhagga Mir and Other Sindhi Proverbs • 113

أَنڌو هاٿِي لشڪر جو زِيانُ

Andho haathee lash^i kar^a jo ziyaan^u

अंधो हाथी लशिकर जो ज़ियानु

Bull in a china shop.

أَنڌو	andho	अंधो	blind
هاٿِي	haathee	हाथी	elephant
لشڪر	lash^i kar^a	लशिकर	army
زِيان	ziyaan^u	ज़ियानु	destruction

سَوَڙِ سارُو پيرَ ڊگھيڙِ

Sawad^i saaroo per^a dighed^i

सवड़ि सारू पेर डिघेड़ि

Cut your coat according to your cloth.

سَوَڙِ	sawad^i	सवडि	quilt
سارُو	saaroo	सारू	according
پير	per^a	पेर	feet
ڊگھيڙِ	dighed^i	डिघेडि	stretch

سَنُ ڳولهي سَنَ کي

San^u golhe san^a khe

सनु गोल्हे सन खे

Birds of a feather flock together.

| سَنُ | san^u | सनु | alike |
| ڳولهي | golhe | गोल्हे | find |

جِتي ماکي، اُتي ڏَنگُ

Jite maakhee, ute dang^u

जिते माखी, उते डंगु

Bees that have honey in their mouths have stings in their tails.

| ماکي | maakhee | माखी | honey |
| ڏَنگُ | dang^u | डंगु | sting |

جِتي گُڙُ، اُتي وِشُ

Jite gud^u, ute vish^u

जिते गुड़ु उते विषु

Beware of those with sweet tongues.

جِتي	jite	जिते	where
گُڙُ	gud^u	गुड़	jaggery
وِشُ	vish^u	विषु	poison

جَڻِيي کان نيپاج ڀلو

J̲aniye khaaⁿ nepaaj^u bhalo

ज़णिये खां नेपाजु भलो

Birth is much but breeding more.

جَڻِيي	j̲aniye	ज़णिये	birth
نيپاجُ	nepaaj^u	नेपाजु	nurture
ڀلو	bhalo	भलो	better

پَنھنجو سو سَھنجو، ٻِيي کان گھُرڻُ ڀه اَھنجو

Peⁿhinjo so sahinjo, b̲iye khaaⁿ ghuran^u bi ahinjo

पंहिंजो सो सहिंजो, बि̱ए खां घुरणु बि अहिंजो

Better spare to have of thine own than ask of others.

سَھنجو	peⁿhinjo	पंहिंजो	mine own
سَھنجو	sahinjo	संहिंजो	easy
ٻِي	b̲iye	बि̱ए	others
اَھنجو	ahinjo	अहिंजो	difficult

ڪِني آڱرِ وَڍي ڀَلي

Kinee aangur[i] vadhee bhalee
किनी आङुरि वढी भली
Better a finger off than always aching.

ڪِني	kinee	किनी	festering
آڱرِ	aangur[i]	आङुरि	finger
وَڍي	vadhee	वढी	cut
ڀَلي	bhalee	भली	better

سُورُ جِنَ يَڄاني

Soor[u] jin[a] bhajaae
सूरु जिन भजाए
Better the tooth out, than always aching.

سُورُ	soor[u]	सूरु	ache
جِنَ	jin[a]	जिन	demons
يَڄاني	bhajaae	भजाए	chase

نادان دوست کان دانا دُشمن ڀلو

Naadaan dost[a] khaa[n], daanaa dushman[u] bhalo
नादान दोस्त खां, दाना दुश्मनु भलो
A wise enemy is better than a foolish friend.

نادان	naadaan	नादान	foolish
ڀَلو	bhalo	भलो	better
دانا	daanaa	दाना	wise
دُشمنُ	dushman[u]	दुश्मनु	enemy

گھرُ ٻاري ڏِياري ڪرڻُ

Ghar^u baare diyaaree karan^u

घरु बारे डियारी करणु

Burn a candle at both ends.

گھَرُ	ghar^u	घरु	home
ٻاري	baare	बारे	burn
ڏِياري	diyaaree	डियारी	Diwali

پِنَڻُ کان پيهَڻُ چڱو

Pinan^u khaaⁿ peehan^u chango

पिनण खां पीहणु चङो

Better wear out shoes than sheets.

پِنَڻُ	pinan^u	पिनण	begging
پيهَڻُ	peehan^u	पीहणु	grind
چڱو	chango	चङो	better

رتُ وِنگو به وَهي

Rat^u vingo bi vahe

रतु विंगो बि वहे

Blood is thicker than water.

رتُ	rat^u	रतु	blood
وِنگو	vingo	विंगो	in all directions

گيهه جو ڏِلو

Geeh^a jo dilo

गीह जो दिलो

Build castles in the air.

گيهه	geeh^a	गीह	clarified butter
ڏِلو	dilo	दिलो	earthen jug

بَه تَه بارِهاںَ

Ba ta baarihaaⁿ

ب त बारिहां

Better a strange companion than alone.*

| بَه | ba | ब | two |
| بارِهاں | baarihaaⁿ | बारिहां | twelve |

عَقُل ري أَدب، گهَٹا جِيئَندين ڈِينهنڑا

Aqulᵃ re adabᵃ, ghanaaⁿ jeeandeⁿ deeⁿhaⁿdaa

अकुल रे अदब, घणा जीअंदें डींहंड़ा

Better be unborn than untaught.

عقل	aqulᵃ	अकुल	wisdom
ري أَدب	re adabᵃ	रे अदब	without wisdom
جِيئَندين	jeeandeⁿ	जीअंदें	live

دَردُ ڈيني، مَلم هَڻُ

Dardᵘ deyee malamᵃ hananᵘ

दर्दु डेई, मलम हणण

Break my head and then give me a plaster.

دَرد	dardᵘ	दर्दु	pain
ڈيني	deyee	डेई	to give
مَلم	malamᵃ	मलम	ointment

سيرَتَ بِنا صُورَتَ کهِڙي

Seeratᵃ binaa sooratᵃ kehidee

सीरत बिना सूरत कहिड़ी

Beauty may have fair leaves, yet bitter fruit.

سيرَتَ	seeratᵃ	सीरत	virtue
بِنا	binaa	बिना	without
صُورَتَ	sooratᵃ	सूरत	beauty

---

*In the old days, people travelled on foot through forests and difficult terrain. They were grateful for even a stranger's company, as the strength of two could equal that of twelve when it came to warding off danger.

دِلِ لَڳي گَڏِي سِي، پَرِي ڪِيا چِيز هُنَه

Dil[i] lagee gadhee se, paree kyaa cheez hai

दिलि लगी गधी से, परी क्या चीज़ है

Beauty lies in the eyes of the beholder.

دِلِ	dil[i]	दिलि	heart
گَڏِي	gadhee	गधी	she-ass
پَرِي	paree	परी	fairy
ڪِيا	kyaa	क्या	what

ذَري تان بَچَڻُ

Zare taa[n] bachan[u]

ज़रे तां बचणु

By the skin of your teeth.

| ذَري | zare | ज़रे | little |
| بَچَڻُ | bachan[u] | बचणु | saved |

سِيرَتَ بِنا صُورَتَ بانسِي

Seerat[a] binaa soorat[a] baa[n]see

सीरत बिना सूरत बांसी

Beauty without virtue is like a flower without fragrance.

سِيرَتَ	seerat[a]	सीरत	virtue
بِنا	binaa	बिना	without
صُورَتَ	soorat[a]	सूरत	beauty
بانسِي	baa[n]see	बांसी	malodorous

جو گَرجي، سو نَه وَرسي

Jo garje, so na varse

जो गर्जे, सो न वर्षे

Barking dogs seldom bite.

| گَرجي | garje | गर्जे | thunder |
| وَرسي | varse | वर्षे | rain |

چورُ نَه تَه چاڪي سَھِين

Chor[u] na ta chaakee sahee[n]

चोरु न त चाकी सहीं

Better a fool than a knave.*

چور	chor[u]	चोर	thief
چاڪي	chaakee	चाकी	simpleton

اَٽي جو ڳوٻاٽو

Ate jo ghobaato

अटे जो घोबाटो

Chinese whispers.

ڳوٻاٽو	ghobaato	घोबाटो	stick, club
اَٽو	ate	अटो	flour

بُري مَتِ، پَرَڻ ۾ پاڻي

Buree mat[i], paran[a] mei[n] paanee

बुरी मति, परण में पाणी

Carry water in a sieve.

بُري مَتِ	buree mat[i]	बुरी मति	bad advice
پَرَڻ	paran[a]	परण	sieve

کَنگھِه ۽ خُونُ، نَه لِڪي سَگھي

Khangh[i] ai[n] khoon[u], na likee saghe

खंघि ऐं ख़ूनु, न लिकी सघे

Cough and killing cannot be hidden.

کَنگھه	khangh[i]	खंघि	cough
خُونُ	khoon[u]	ख़ूनु	murder
لِڪي	likee	लिकी	hide

---

*Japanese proverb

کِنُ کِنَ سان
نه ڌوپي

Kin^u, kin^a saa^n na dhope

किनु, किन सां न धोपे

Cleaning a blot with blotted fingers maketh a greater blur.

| کِنُ | kin^u | किनु | dirt |
| ڌوپي | dhope | धोपे | wash |

پاڻيءَ کان اڳُ
ڪپڙا نه لاهِه

Paanee^a khaa^n ag^u kap^{i}daa na laah^i

पाणी^{a} खां अगु कपिड़ा न लाहि

Catch a bear before you sell its skin.

پاڻي	paanee^a	पाणी	water
اَڳُ	ag^u	अगु	prior
لاهِه	laah^i	लाहि	shed

صُورَتَ کان
سِيرَتَ ڀلي

Soorat^a khaa^n seerat^a bhalee

सूरत खां सीरत भली

Choose a wife by your ear, rather than your eye.*

| صُورَتَ | soorat^a | सूरत | looks, beauty |
| سِيرَتَ | seerat^a | सीरत | manners, behaviour |

---

*Japanese proverb

سُتا سُورَ جاڳائڻُ

Sutaa soor[a] jaagaain[u]

सुता सूर जाग़ाइणु

Reopen old wounds.

سُتا	sutaa	सुता	sleeping
سُورَ	soor[a]	सूर	pain
جاڳائڻُ	jaagaain[u]	जाग़ाइणु	awaken

ڪَپڙي آهرِ وَڳو ناهِه

Kap[i]de aahir[i] vago thaah[i]

कपिड़े आहिरि वग़ो ठाहि

Cut your coat according to your cloth.

| آهرِ | aahir[i] | आहिरि | according |
| وَڳو | vago | वग़ो | dress |

مِمِٽي سِپَ

Miminee sip[a]

मिमिणी सिप

Still waters run deep.

| مِمِٽي سِپَ | miminee sip[a] | मिमिणी सिप | closed shell |

اُبُ اَکِنين پيو ڏِسِجي

Ubh[u] akhie[n] piyo dis[i]je

उभु अखिएं पियो ड़िसिजे

Clear as crystal.

اُبُ	ubh[u]	उभु	sky
اَکِنين	akhie[n]	अखिएं	eyes
ڏِسِجي	dis[i]je	ड़िसिजे	see

گھر جي سَهيڙُ، دانَ بَرابرِ

Ghar[a] jee sahed[a], daan[a] baraabar[i]

घर जी सहेड़, दान बराबरि

Charity begins at home.

گھرَ	ghar[a]	घर	home
سَهيڙُ	sahed[a]	सहेड	frugality
دان	daan[a]	दान	charity

نيڪي ڪرِ، دَرياهه ۾ ٻوڙِ

Nekee kar[i], dariyaah[a] mei[n] <u>b</u>od[i]

नेकी करि, दरियाह में बोड़ि

When doing charity, let your left hand not know what your right hand does.

نيڪي	nekee	नेकी	good deed, charity
درياهه	dariyaah[a]	दरियाह	ocean, river
ٻوڙِ	<u>b</u>od[i]	बोड़ि	drown

ٻَٻُرَ چا جاڻَنِ ٻيرِنِ مان

<u>B</u>abur[a] chhaa jaanan[i] <u>b</u>eran[i] maa[n]

बबुर छा जाणनि बेरनि मां

Don't ask the elm tree for pears.

ٻَٻُر	<u>b</u>abur[a]	बबुर	brambles
جاڻَنِ	jaanan[i]	जाणनि	know
ٻيرِنِ	<u>b</u>eran[i]	बेर	berries

Aaya Pir, Bhagga Mir and Other Sindhi Proverbs

آزِمائي کي جو
آزِمائي
سو ڏوڙِ مُنھَن
مِ پائي

Aaz'maae khe jo aaz'maae, so dhood' munh[an] mei[n] paae

आज़िमाए खे जो आज़िमाए, सो धूड़ि मुंहं में पाए

Fool me once, shame on you; fool me twice, shame on me.

| آزِمائي | aaz'maae | आज़िमाए | experienced |

پَنھِنجي ڪَڏَ
کوٽَڻُ

Pe[n]hinjee khad[a] khotan[u]

पंहिंजी खड़ खोटणु

Dig your own grave.

| ڪَڏَ | khad[a] | खड़ | pit |
| کوٽَڻُ | khotan[u] | खोटणु | dig |

جِتي پُڄَڻُ ڪَمُ
ناھي
اُتي ڀَڄَڻُ ڪَمُ
وَرِيام جو

Jite pujan[u] kam[u] naahe, ute bhajan[u] kam[u] variyaam jo

जिते पुजणु कमु नाहे, उते भजणु कमु वरियाम जो

Discretion is the better part of valour.

پُڄَڻُ	pujan[u]	पुजणु	to cope with
ڀَڄَڻُ	bhajan[u]	भजणु	run away
وَرِيام	variyaam	वरियाम	brave

سونار جا سَوَ
(ڍَکَ)، لوهار
جو هِکُ
(ڍَکُ)

Sonaar[a] jaa sav[a] (dhak[a]), lohaar[a] jo hik[u] (dhak[u])

सोनार जा सव (ढक), लोहार जो हिकु (ढकु)

Deliver your words not by number but by weight.

سونار	sonaar[a]	सोनार	goldsmith
سَوَ	sav[a]	सव	hundred
ڍَکَ	dhak[a]	ढक	strokes
لوهار	lohaar[a]	लोहार	ironsmith

مِٺي ڀہ ماٺِ،
مُٺي ڀہ ماٺِ

Mithee bi maath[i], muthee bi maath[i]

मिठी बि माठि, मुठी बि माठि

Damned if I do and damned if I don't.

مِٺي	mithee	मिठी	sweet
ماٺِ	maath[i]	माठि	quiet
مُٺي	muthee	मुठी	harsh

مَولا مِينهُن وَساءِ

Maulaa meenh[un] vasaai

मौला मींहुं वसाइ

If hard work is the key to success, most people would rather pick the lock.

| مَولا | maulaa | मौला | lord |
| مِينهُن | meenh[un] | मींहुं | rain |

رِدَ چا جاڻي
رَباب مان

Ridh^a chhaa jaane rabaab^a maaⁿ

रिढ छा जाणे, रबाब मां

Did you ever hear an ass play a lute or a lyre.

رِدِ	ridh[a]	रिढ	sheep
جاڻي	jaane	जाणे	knows
رَباب	rabaab[a]	रबाब	musical instrument

دُورِ باش،
خوُش باش

Door[i] baash, khush baash

दूरि बाश, खुश बाश

Distance makes the heart grow fonder.

دُورِ	door[i]	दूरि	away
باش	baash	बाश	be
خوُش	khush	खुश	happy

راتِ جوُن
گالھِيوُن، ڏِينِھَن
جو نَہ پَرَنِ

Raat[i] joo[n] gaalh[i]yoo[n], dee[n]h[an] jo na paran[i]

राति जूं गाल्हियूं, ड़ींहं जो न परनि

Don't look for this year's birds in last year's nest.

راتِ	raat[i]	राति	night
گالھِيوُن	gaalh[i]yoo[n]	गाल्हियूं	talks
پَرَنِ	paran[i]	परनि	equate

ڊُڌو کِيرُ ٿَڻين
نَه پَوي

Dudho kheer[u] thane[n] na pave

डुधो खीरु थणें न पवे

Do not cry over spilt milk.

ڊُڌو	dudho	डुधो	milked, extracted
کِيرُ	kheer[u]	खीरु	milk
ٿَڻين	thane[n]	थणें	udders

پَرائي ماڙي
ڏِسي، پَنھنجي
ڀُونگي نَه
ڊاھِجي

Paraaee maadee disee, pe[n]hinjee bhoongee na daah[i]je

पराई माड़ी डिसी, पंहिजी भूंगी न डाहिजे

Don't envy the harvest of the rich, envy their planting.

پَرائي	paraaee	पराई	others'
ماڙي	maadee	माड़ी	mansion
ڀُونگي	bhoongee	भूंगी	humble dwelling
ڊاھِجي	daah[i]je	डाहिजे	destroy

ھَٺُ ڪُٺائي حَلوا
کائٿُ

Hat[u] khutaae halvaa khaain[u]

हटु खुटाए हल्वा खाइणु

Don't let your jaws overrun your claws.*

ھَٺُ ڪُٺائي	hat[u] khutaae	हटु खुटाए	bankruptcy
حَلوا	halvaa	हल्वा	sweetmeat

---

*Cheshire proverb, 1917

ماءُ ٻارَ کي
کيرُ ڀِه ري
گهُرِيو نَه ڏِني

Maau baarᵃ khe kheerᵘ bi re ghurⁱyo na diye
माउ बार खे खीरु बि रे घुर्यो न डिए
The crying baby gets the milk.

| ري گهُرِيو | re ghurⁱyo | रे घुर्यो | without asking |

پاڻَ سان ڀيٽَ
نَه ڪَرِ

Paanᵃ saaⁿ bhetᵃ na karⁱ
पाण सां भेट न करि
Do not tar him with the same brush.

| ڀيٽَ | bhetᵃ | भेट | liken, compare |

ڏِيَڻَ کان
ڏيکارَڻُ ڀَلو

Diyanᵃ khaaⁿ dekhaaranᵘ bhalo
डियण खां डेखारणु भलो
Give a man a fish and you feed him for a day; teach a man to fish and you feed him for a lifetime.

| ڏِيَڻَ | diyanᵃ | डियण | give |
| ڏيکارَڻُ | dekhaaranᵘ | डेखारणु | show |

سُٿِرو آيلُ
سُٿِرو وَڃي
(ناڻو)

Suthⁱro aayalᵘ, suthⁱro vanye (naano)
सुथिरो आयलु, सुथिरो वञे (नाणो)
Easy come, easy go.

| سُٿِرو | suthⁱro | सुथिरो | easy, accessible |
| ناڻو | naano | नाणो | money |

سَڀ ڪَنھِن کي پَنھنجو آواز مِٺو لڳي

Sabh⁽ᵃ⁾ keⁿhiⁿkhe peⁿhinjo aawaaz⁽ᵘ⁾ mitho lage
सभ कंहिखे पंहिंजो आवाजु मिठो लगे

Each bird loves to hear itself sing.

سَڀ ڪَنھِنکي	sabh⁽ᵃ⁾ keⁿhiⁿkhe	सभ कंहिखे	everybody
پَنھنجو	peⁿhinjo	पंहिंजो	own
آواز	aawaaz⁽ᵘ⁾	आवाजु	voice
مِٺو	mitho	मिठो	sweet

سَڀَ م چَڱائي

Sabh⁽ᵃ⁾ meⁿ changaaee
सभ में चङाई

Every cloud has a silver lining.

سَڀَ	sabh⁽ᵃ⁾	सभ	all
چَڱائي	changaaee	चङाई	good

سَڀِني جو وارو وَري

Sabhⁱnee jo vaaro vare
सभिनी जो वारो वरे

Every dog has his day.

وارو	vaaro	वारो	turn
وَري	vare	वरे	comes

سَڀِڪو پَنھنجو ٻوٽو ٻاري

Sabhⁱko peⁿhinjo <u>b</u>ooto <u>b</u>aare
सभिको पंहिंजो बूटो बारे

Every miller draws water to his own mill.

ٻوٽو	<u>b</u>ooto	बूटो	bush
ٻاري	<u>b</u>aare	बारे	burn, alight

تَنَ جو گھاءُ
يَرِجي وَڃي،
پَرَ خواريءَ
جي عُمِرِ لَنبي

Tanᵃ jo ghaau bharⁱjee vanye, parᵃ khwaareeᵃ jee umirⁱ lambee

तन जो घाउ भरिजी वञे, पर ख़्वारीᵃ जी उमिरि लंबी

An evil wound is soon cured but not an evil name.

| خواري | khwaareeᵃ | ख़्वारी | defamation |
| لَنبي | lambee | लंबी | long |

اُدَمَ کي بِہ پَرَ آهِنِ

Udamᵃ khe bi parᵃ aahinⁱ

उदम खे बि पर आहिनि

Effort leads to success.*

| اُدَمَ | udamᵃ | उदम | effort |
| پَرَ | parᵃ | पर | wings |

سِياڻي لاءِ أَکِ جو اِشارو

Siyaane laai akhⁱ jo ishaaro

सियाणे लाइ अखि जो इशारो

A word to the wise.

| سِياڻي | siyaane | सियाणे | wise person |
| اِشارو | ishaaro | इशारो | sign |

کوُھہ ۾ ڊيڏَرُ

Khoohᵃ meiⁿ dedarᵘ

खूह में डेडरु

Frog in the well.

| کوُھہ | khoohᵃ | खूह | well |
| ڊيڏَرُ | dedarᵘ | डेडरु | frog |

---

*Cheshire proverb, 15th century

پھِرِيون مُلھُه،
ڪَستُوۡرِي

Pah'r'yon mulh^u, khastooree

पहिरियों मुल्हु, खस्तूरी

First price, best price.

| | مُلھُه | mulh^u | मुल्हु | price |

جاننٿي جو ڀاڳُ
کِڻ ۾ وَري

Jaanthe jo bhaag^u khin^a meiⁿ vare

जांठे जो भागु खिन में वरे

Fortune favours the brave.

| جاننٿي | jaanthe | जांठे | muscular |
| ڀاڳُ | bhaag^u | भागु | fate |

سياڻا ڀُوڪَنِ
جا گھرَ وَسائيِنِ

Siyaanaa bhookanⁱ, jaa ghar^a vasaaeenⁱ

सियाणा भूकनि, जा घर वसाईनि

Fools make houses, wise men live in them.

| سياڻا | siyaanaa | सियाणा | wise |
| ڀُوڪَنِ | bhookanⁱ | भूकनि | fools |

مُنھُن ڊِسِي
تِلکُ ڊِيَڻُ

Munh^{un} <u>d</u>isee tilk^u <u>d</u>iyan^u

मुंहुं डिसी तिल्कु डियणु

To judge a book by its cover.

| مُنھُن | munh^{un} | मुंहुं | face |

پَنھنجي کائيءَ
۾ ڪِرَڻُ

Peⁿhinjee khaaee^a meiⁿ kiran^u

पंहिंजी खाईअ में किरणु

Fall into your own grave.

| کائيءَ | khaaee^a | खाई | ditch |
| ڪِرَڻُ | kiran^u | किरणु | fall |

بَسِياري خواري

Basⁱyaaree khwaaree

बसियारी ख़्वारी

Familiarity breeds contempt.

بَسِياري	basⁱyaaree	बसियारी	familiarity
خواري	khwaaree	ख़्वारी	ill feeling

بُڈَلَ بيڑِيءَ جو لوهُه بِه چِڱو

B<u>ud</u>al^a <u>b</u>edee^a jo loh^u bi chango

बुडल बेड़ीअ जो लोहु बि चङो

From a bad paymaster, get what you can.

بُڈَلَ بيڑِي	<u>b</u>u<u>d</u>al^a <u>b</u>edee^a	बुडल बेड़ी	sunk boat
لوهُه	lohu	लोहु	iron

دِلِ جي ماپَ وَاتَ مان مِلي

Dilⁱ jee maap^a vaat^a maaⁿ mile

दिलि जी माप वात मां मिले

The face is the index of the heart.

دِلِ	dilⁱ	दिलि	heart
ماپَ	maap^a	माप	measure
وَاتَ	vaat^a	वात	mouth

جَهڙو چَراغُ تَهڙو چَرڪُ، ٻولي ٻوليءَ جو فَرقُ

Jehⁱdo charaag^u tehⁱdo chark^u, <u>b</u>olee <u>b</u>olee^a jo farq^u

जहिड़ो चरागु तहिड़ो चर्कु, बोली बोलीअ जो फ़र्कु

Goose, gander and gosling are three sounds but one thing.

چَراغُ	charaag^u	चरागु	lamp
چَرڪُ	chark^u	चर्कु	lantern
فَرقُ	farq^u	फ़र्कु	difference

سائينءَ وَٽِ
دير آهي، پَرَ
اَنڌيرُ ڪونهي

Saaee^{n-a} vatⁱ derⁱ aahe, par^a andher^u konhe

साईंअ वटि देरि आहे, पर अंधेरु कोन्हे

God is fair and just.

سائينِ	saaee^{n-a}	साईं	Lord
دير	derⁱ	देरि	late
اَنڌيرُ	andher^u	अंधेरु	injustice

سائينءَ جي دَ
رَ تي توبَهَ

Saaee^{n-a} je dar^a te tobah^a

साईंअ जे दर ते तोबह

Repent then, and turn to God.

| توبَهَ | tobah^a | तोबह | repent |

مارَڻ واري
کان جيئارَڻ
وارو وَڏو

Maaran^a vaare khaaⁿ jeeaaran^a vaaro va<u>d</u>o

मारण वारे खां जीआरण वारो वडो

One who gives life is greater than one who kills.

| مارَڻ واري | maaran^a vaare | मारण वारे | killer |
| جيئارَڻ | jeeaaran^a | जीआरण | to give life |

جَنھن ساسُ
ڏِنو، اُهو
گِراسُ ڀِ ڏِيندو

Jenhⁱⁿ saas^u <u>d</u>ino, uho giraas^u bi <u>d</u>eendo

जंहिं सासु डिनो, उहो ग्रासु बि डींदो

God sends cold after clothes.

| ساسُ | saas^u | सासु | life |
| گِراسُ | giraas^u | ग्रासु | food |

بَندي جي مَنَ ۾ هِڪِڙي صاحِب جي مَنَ ۾ ٻِي

Bande je man^a meiⁿ hikⁱdee, Saahib^a je man^a meiⁿ bee

बंदे जे मन में हिकिड़ी, साहिब जे मन में ब़ी

Man proposes, God disposes.

بَندي	bande	बंदे	human being
صاحِب	saahib^a	साहिब	God

يَتُ ڏيني لَٺِ هَڻُ

Bhat^u deyee, lathⁱ hanan^u

भतु ड़ेई लठि हणणु

Give me a roast and then beat me with the spit.

يَتُ	bhat^u	भतु	porridge
لَٺِ	lathⁱ	लठि	baton

ڏي نَه، تَه ڏُکوءِ تَه نَه

De na, ta dukhoi ta na

ड़े न, त ड़ुखोइ त न

Help not, hurt not.

ڏُکوءِ	dukhoi	ड़ुखोइ	hurt

ڏايو سو گابو

Daadho so gaabo

ड़ाढो सो गाबो

Might is right.

ڏايو	daadho	ड़ाढो	strong, brave
گابو	gaabo	गाबो	correct

سائیِن مِلِیو،
سَڀُ مِلِیو

Saaeeⁿ milⁱyo, sabh^u milⁱyo

साई मिलियो, सभु मिलियो

If God is all you have, you have all you need.

سائیِن	saaeeⁿ	साई	God
مِلِیو	milⁱyo	मिलियो	got
سَڀُ	sabh^u	सभु	everything

عَقلُ جو ڪُپو

Aqul^a jo kupo

अकुल जो कुपो

He has as much wit as three folks—two fools and a madman.*

| عَقلُ | aqul^a | अकुल | wisdom |
| ڪُپو | kupo | कुपो | airhead |

ناڻا گھوڙِیا
سِرَنِ تان
سِرَ گھوڙِیا
شَرمَنِ تان

Naanaa ghoriyaa siranⁱ taaⁿ, sir^a ghoriyaa sharmanⁱ taaⁿ

नाणा घोरिया सिरनि तां, सिर घोरिया शर्मनि तां

Spend your money to save your life, but give your life to save your honour.

ناڻا	naanaa	नाणा	money
سِرَ	sir^a	सिर	head
شَرمَنِ	sharmanⁱ	शर्मनि	honour

---

*Cheshire proverb

َدڽُ تَه دَڽِي، نَه
تَه وِكُڻُ كَڻِي

Dhan[u] ta dhanee, na ta vikun[u] khanee

धणु त धणी, न त विकुणु खणी

He that by the plough would thrive must either hold or drive.

دَڽُ	dhan[u]	धणु	livestock
دَڽِي	dhanee	धणी	owner
وِكُڻُ	vikun[u]	विकुणु	sell

مُلكُ مَتِيو تاں
گھوريو، شالَ
مالِكُ نَه مَڽِي

Mulk[u] mat[i]yo taa[n] ghoriyo, shaal[a] maalik[u] na mate

मुल्कु मतियो तां घोरियो, शाल मालिकु न मटे

He loseth nothing that loseth not the Lord.*

| مالِكُ | maalik[u] | मालिकु | Lord |
| مَڽِي | mate | मटे | turn away from |

مَكَّڻَ جِي شِيخَ
پَچائِڻُ

Makhan[a] jee sheekh[a] pachaain[u]

मखण जी शीख़ पचाइणु

To roast snow in a furnace.

مَكَّڻَ	makhan[a]	मखण	butter
شِيخَ	sheekh[a]	शीख़	rod, skewer
پَچائِڻُ	pachaain[u]	पचाइणु	roast

*Old English proverb

كَكَ جو چورُ، لَكَ جو چورُ

Kakh^a jo chor^u, lakh^a jo chor^u

कख जो चोरु, लख जो चोरु

He who steals a calf, will steal a cow.

| كَكَ | kakh^a | कख | straw |
| لَكَ | lakh^a | लख | hundred thousand |

سَپُ نَه ماري، سَپَ جو سراپُ ماري

Sap^u na maare, sap^a jo saraap^u maare

सपु न मारे, सप जो सरापु मारे

He that fears danger always feels it.

| سَپُ | sap^a | सप | snake |
| سَراپُ | saraap^u | सरापु | curse |

لِکِيو پَري، پَرَ کَڎهِن نَه ٽَري

Likh^{i}yo pare, par^a kad^{a}hi^n na tare

लिखियो परे, पर कड़हिं न टरे

He that is born to be hanged will never be drowned.

لِکِيو	likh^{i}yo	लिखियो	destiny
پَري	pare	परे	distant
ٽَري	tare	टरे	change slightly

باندَرُ چا ڄاڻي سُنڍِ جو سَوادُ

Baandar⁽ᵘ⁾ chhaa jaane sundh⁽ⁱ⁾ jo sawaad⁽ᵘ⁾

बांदरु छा जाणे सुंढि जो सवादु

Honey is not for an ass's mouth.

باندَرُ	baandar⁽ᵘ⁾	बांदरु	monkey
جاڻي	jaane	जाणे	knows
سُنڍِ	sundh⁽ⁱ⁾	सुंढि	dried ginger
سَوادُ	sawaad⁽ᵘ⁾	सवादु	taste

ديگِ اُڀامي، تَه پَنھنجا ڪَنا ساڙي

Deg⁽ⁱ⁾ ubhaame, ta pe⁽ⁿ⁾hinjaa kanaa saade

देगि उभामे, त पंहिंजा कना साड़े

He that mischief hatches, mischief catches.

ديگِ	deg⁽ⁱ⁾	देगि	earthen vessel
اُڀامي	ubhaame	उभामे	boil over
ڪَنا	kanaa	कना	rims, edges

تِرَ جي ڳُٿي، سَوَ چوٽُون کائي

Tir⁽ᵃ⁾ jee guthee, sav⁽ᵃ⁾ chotoo⁽ⁿ⁾ khaae

तिर जी गुथी, सव चोटूं खाए

For want of a nail, the kingdom was lost.

تِرَ	tir⁽ᵃ⁾	तिर	a sesame seed
ڳُٿي	guthee	गुथी	missed
سَوَ	sav⁽ᵃ⁾	सव	hundred
چوٽُون	chotoo⁽ⁿ⁾	चोटूं	injuries

تَڪَڙِ ڪَمُ شيطانَ جو

Takad⁽ⁱ⁾ kam⁽ᵘ⁾ shetaan⁽ᵃ⁾ jo

तकड़ि कमु शैतान जो

Haste is of the devil.

| تَڪَڙِ | takad⁽ⁱ⁾ | तकड़ि | haste |
| شيطانَ | shetaan⁽ᵃ⁾ | शैतान | demon |

سيءَ مِ گڏهَ
جا آٺَرَ بہ چڱّا

See[a] mei[n] ga_dah_[a] jaa aathar[a] bi changaa

सी[अ] में गड़ह जा आथर बि चङा

Hunger seasons all dishes.*

سيءَ	see[a]	सी[अ]	cold
گڏهَ	ga_dah_[a]	गड़ह	donkey
آٺَرَ	aathar[a]	आथर	cloth coverings

بُکَ بُچڙي ٽولَ
لاءِ بہ واہَ واہَ
ڪَري

Bukh[a] buchhide tol[a] laai bi vaah[a] vaah[a] kare

बुख बुछिड़े टोल लाइ बि वाह वाह करे

Hungry dogs eat dirty puddings.

| ٽولَ | tol[a] | टोल | snack |
| واہَ واہَ | vaah[a] vaah[a] | वाह वाह | appreciation |

بُکَ بُچڙي،
دانا ديوانا
ڪَري

Bukh[a] buchhidee, daanaa deevaanaa kare

बुख बुछिड़ी, दाना दीवाना करे

Hunger breaks through stone walls.

بُکَ	bukh[a]	बुख	hunger
بُچڙي	buchhidee	बुछिड़ी	pernicious
دانا	daanaa	दाना	sane
ديوانا	deevaanaa	दीवाना	insane

---

*A donkey may be a smelly animal, but in winter, even its cloth covering is better than none at all.

بُکَ مِ بَصَرَ
بہ مِنا

Bukh^a meiⁿ basar^a bi mithaa

बुख में बसर बि मिठा

Hunger finds no fault with cookery.*

بُکَ	bukh^a	बुख	hunger
بَصَرَ	basar^a	बसर	onions
مِنا	mithaa	मिठा	sweet

سَچَ کي نَہ
لَهَرَ، نَہ لوڏو

Sach^a khe na lahar^a, na lo<u>d</u>o

सच खे न लहर, न लोड़ो

Honesty is the best policy.

سَچَ	sach^a	सच	truth
لَهَرَ نَہ	lahar^a, na	लहर न	unshakeable
لوڏو	lo<u>d</u>o	लोड़ो	

جَهڙي سِيرَتَ،
تَهڙي صُورَتَ

Jehⁱdee seerat^a, tehⁱdee soorat^a

जहिड़ी सीरत, तहिड़ी सूरत

Handsome is as handsome does.

| سِيرَتَ | seerat^a | सीरत | manner |
| صُورَتَ | soorat^a | सूरत | looks |

نانگُ بہ مَري
ءِ لَٺِ بہ نَہ
ڀَڃي

Naang^u bi mare aiⁿ lathⁱ bi na bha<u>j</u>e

नांगु बि मरे एं लठि बि न भज़े

Have your cake and eat it too.

نانگُ	naang^u	नांग	snake
لَٺِ	lathⁱ	लठि	stick
ڀَڃي	bha<u>j</u>e	भजे	break

---

*Japanese proverb

پَنھنجو گَھرُ،
گُروءَ جو دَرُ

Pe^nhinjo ghar^u, Guroo^a jo dar^u

पंहिंजो घरु, गुरूअ जो दरु

Home is home, be it ever so homely.

گَھرُ	ghar^u	घरु	home
گُروءَ	guroo^a	गुरूअ	God
دَرُ	dar^u	दरु	door

چاھَہ سَچائيءَ
جي، پَرَ راھَہ
بُرائيءَ جي

Chaah^a sachaaee^a jee, par^a raah^a buraaee^a jee

चाह सचाईअ जी, पर राह बुराईअ जी

The road to hell is paved with good intentions.

چاھَہ	chaah^a	चाह	desire
سَچائي	sachaaee^a	सचाई	honesty
راھَہ	raah^a	राह	path
بُرائي	buraaee^a	बुराई	bad deed

کَنِيِنۡ کَپي
کانَہ، گولھي
لَڀي کانَہ

Kha^nee^n khape kaan^a, golhee labhe kaan^a

खंई खपे कान, गोल्ही लभे कान

He who seeks what he should not, finds what he would not.

کَنِيِنۡ	kha^nee^n	खंई	available
گولھي	golhee	गोल्ही	seek
لَڀي	labhe	लभे	find

ٻار کي روئڻ | Baarᵃ khe ruanᵃ binaa maau bi khaadho na diye
بِنا ماءُ ڀه کاڌو
نَه ڏِني
بार खे रुअणᵃ बिना माउ बि खाधो न ड़िए

The squeaky wheel gets the oil.

ٻار	baarᵃ	बार	child
روئَڻُ بِنا	ruanᵃ binaa	रुअणᵃ बिना	without crying
کاڌو	khaadho	खाधो	food

اِنسانُ تَه نِسِيانُ | Insaanᵘ ta nisiyaanᵘ
इंसानु त निसियानु

To err is human.

| اِنسانُ | insaanᵘ | इंसानु | human |
| نِسِيانُ | nisiyaanᵘ | निसियान | careless |

جِتي سَتياناسِ، | Jite satyaanaasⁱ, ute sawaa satyaanaasⁱ
اُتي سَوا
سَتياناسِ
जिते सत्यानासि, उते सवा सत्यानासि

In for a penny, in for a pound.

| سَتياناسِ | satyaanaasⁱ | सत्यानासि | ruination |
| سَوا | sawaa | सवा | one and a quarter |

بيڪاريءَ کان | Bekaareeᵃ khaaⁿ begaaree bhalee
بيگاري ڀَلي
बेकारीᵃ खां बेगारी भली

Better to do something than to do nothing.

بيڪاري	bekaareeᵃ	बेकारी	jobless
بيگاري	begaaree	बेगारी	forced labour
ڀَلي	bhalee	भली	better

مالِكُ ڏِنِي تَہ
ڇَپَرُ ڦاڙي ڏِنِي

Maaliku diye ta chhaparu phaade diye

मालिकु डिए त छपरु फाड़े डिए

It never rains but it pours.

مالِكُ	maaliku	मालिकु	Lord
ڇَپَرُ	chhaparu	छपरु	roof

آئي ٽانڊي کي،
بورِچياڻي ٿي
ويٺي

Aaee taande khe, bor'chiyaanee thee vethee

आई टांडे खे, बोरिचियाणी थी वेठी

Give them an inch and they will take a mile.

ٽانڊو	taande	टांडे	coal
بورِچياڻي	bor'chiyaanee	बोरिचियाणी	lady cook

پَرائي ڌُهِلين،
اَحۡمَقُ نَچي

Paraae duhile[n], ah'maqu nache

पराए दुहिलें, अहिमकु नचे

It is easy to cry Yule at other people's cost.

پَرائي	paraae	पराए	other
ڌُهِلين	duhile[n]	दुहिलें	festivity
اَحۡمَقُ	ah'maqu	अहिमकु	fool
نَچي	nache	नचे	dances

آزۡمائي کي
آزۡمائي، سو
دوکو کائي

Aaz'maae khe aaz'maae, so dokho khaae

आज़िमाए खे आज़िमाए, सो दोखो खाए

It is a silly fish that is caught twice with the same bait.

آزۡمائي	aaz'maae	आज़िमाए	tried
دوکو	dokho	दोखो	fooled

تاڙي ٻه هٿي وَڄي

Taadee bi-hathee vaje
ताड़ी बि हथी वजे
It takes two to tango.

تاڙي	taadee	ताड़ी	clap
ٻه هٿي	bi-hathee	बि हथी	two hands

هَماري ٻِلي، هَماري کو ڪاتي

Hamaaree bilee, hamaare ko kaate
हमारी बिली, हमारे को काटे
I taught you to swim and now you drown me.

ٻِلي	bilee	बिली	cat
هَماري	hamaaree	हमारी	mine
ڪاتي	kaate	काटे	bite

اَنڌَنِ م ڪاڻو راجا

Andhan^i mei^n kaano raajaa
अंधनि में काणो राजा
In the kingdom of the blind, the one-eyed man is king.

اَنڌَنِ	andhan^i	अंधनि	blind persons
ڪاڻو	kaano	काणो	one-eyed

جوٺِ ڪي مايا، پَراڄَتِ جايا

Jooth^i kee maayaa, paraachhat^i jaayaa
जूठि की माया, पराछति जाया
Ill-gotten gains never prosper.

جوٺِ	jooth^i	जूठि	fake
پَراڄَتِ	paraachhat^i	पराछति	repentance

نَه ڪَنهنجي
ڪَٽِي کي هَٿُ
لائِجي،
نَه پَنهنجو پَٽُ
ڦاڙائِجي

Na keⁿhinje khathe khe hath^u laaije, na peⁿhinjo pat^u phaadaaije

न कंहिंजे खथे खे हथु लाइजे, न पंहिंजो पटु फाड़ाइजे

Put not your hand between the bark and the tree.

| ڪَٽِي | khathe | खथे | hand-woven woollen coverlet |
| پَٽُ | pat^u | पटु | untwisted silk |

عِشقَ ءِ عَقُلَ
جي ٿِي نَه
ڀائِيواري

Ishq^a aiⁿ aqul^a jee thie na bhaaeewaaree

इश्क़ ऐं अक़ुल जी थिए न भाईवारी

It is impossible to love and be wise.

عِشقَ	ishq^a	इश्क़	love
عَقُلَ	aqul^a	अक़ुल	wisdom
ڀائِيواري	bhaaeewaa-ree	भाईवारी	partnership

سَڀُ (جِيوَ)
ڀَڳوانَ جا گُل

Sabh^u (jeev^a) Bhagwaan^a jaa gul^a

सभु (जीव) भग॒वान जा गु॒ल

It takes all kinds to make this world.

سَڀُ	sabh^u	सभु	everyone
ڀَڳوانَ	Bhagwaan^a	भग॒वान	God
گُل	gul^a	गु॒ल	flowers

Aaya Pir, Bhagga Mir and Other Sindhi Proverbs • 145

کِنو عُضوو
کَٹیَلُ ڀَلو

Kino uzvo katiyal[u] bhalo

किनो उज़्वो कटियलु भलो

If thy right eye offend thee, pluck it out.

عُضوو	uzvo	उज़्वो	limb, organ
کِنو	kino	किनो	bad, infected
کَٹیَلُ	katiyal[u]	कटियलु	cut

گھِسِيوُن گھي
جِيَنَّ ڪان
شانَ سان مَرَنُ
چَڱو

Gheesiyoo[n] gahee jeean[a] khaa[n] shaan[a] saa[n] maran[u] chango

घीसियूं गही जीअण खां शान सां मरणु चङो

It is better to die on your feet than live on your knees.

گھِسِيوُن	gheesiyoo[n]	घीसियूं	crawl
جِيَنَّ	jeean[a]	जीअण	live life
شانَ	shaan[a]	शान	honour
مَرَنُ	maran[u]	मरणु	death

ڏُکُ ۽ سُکُ
سَڱا ڀاءُر

Dukh[u] ain sukh[u] sagaa bhaaur[a]

दुखु ऐं सुखु सगा भाउर

Joy and sorrow are next door neighbours.

ڏُکُ	dukh[u]	दुखु	sorrow
سُکُ	sukh[u]	सुखु	joy
سَڱا ڀاءُر	sagaa bhaaur[a]	सगा भाउर	blood brothers

اَئو کاڌو کوُئي، ماَرَ پيئي گابي تي

Ato khaadho kooe, maar[a] peyee gaabe te

अटो खाधो कूए, मार पेई गाबे ते

January commits the fault, and May bears the blame.

| کوُئي | kooe | कूए | mouse |
| گابي | gaabe | गाबे | calf |

کوُئي لَڏي هَنڊَ ڊَ ري، چي : آنءُ بہ پَساري

Kooe ladhee haid[a] zaree, che : aau^n bi pasaaree

कूए लधी हैड ज़री, चे : आउं बि पसारी

Become too big for your boots.

| آنءُ | aau^n | आउं | I |
| پَساري | pasaaree | पसारी | trader |

نوُنٺِ لَڳي، ساهِڙي ڀَڄي

Thoonth[i] lagee, saahidee bhagee

ठूंठि लगी, साहिड़ी भगी

Make a mountain out of a molehill.

نوُنٺِ	thoonth[i]	ठूंठि	elbow
لَڳي	lagee	लगी	touch
ساهِڙي	saahidee	साहिड़ी	friend
ڀَڄي	bhagee	भगी	ran away

ايڪ پَنڌِ، دو ڪارج

Ek pandh[i], do kaarj[i]

एक पंधि, दो कार्जि

Kill two birds with one stone.

| ايڪ پَنڌِ | ek pandh[i] | एक पंधि | one trip |
| دو ڪارج | do kaarj[i] | दो कार्जि | two jobs |

Aaya Pir, Bhagga Mir and Other Sindhi Proverbs • 147

مُحِبَتَ نَہ ڈِسي بُرائي

Mohibata na dise buraaee

मुहिबत न ड़िसे बुराई

Love is blind.

مُحِبَتَ	mohibata	मुहिबत	love
بُرائي	buraaee	बुराई	vice

أُهو سونُ ئي گهوريو، جو ڪَنَ چِني

Uho sonu ee ghoriyo, jo kana chhine

उहो सोनु ई घोरियो, जो कन छिने

Lean liberty is better than fat slavery.

سونُ	sonu	सोनु	gold, wealth
ڪَنَ چِني	kana chhine	कन छिने	split earlobe

عِشقَ ۽ عَقُلَ جي ٿي نَہ آشنائي

Ishqa ain aqula jee thee na aashnaaee

इश्क़ ऐं अकुल जी थी न आश्नाई

Love and knowledge do not live together.

عِشقَ	ishqa	इश्क़	love
عَقُلَ	aqula	अकुल	wisdom
آشنائي	aashnaaee	आश्नाई	companionship

148 • Sindh Bani

پَڙھَڻُ، تَرَڻُ، تيرَ
هَڻُ، چوٺِين
سُواري، ننڍي
هوُندي جو نَه
سِکِيو، وَڏي
هوُندي خواري

Padhan{u}, taran{u}, teer{a} hanan{u}, chothee{n} suwaaree, nandhe hoonde jo na sikhiyo vade hoonde khuwaaree

पढ़णु, तरणु, तीर हणणु, चोथीं सुवारी, नंढे हूंदे जो न सिखियो, वड़े हूंदे खुवारी

Learnt young is hard to lose.

پَڙھَڻُ	padhan{u}	पढ़णु	reading
تَرَڻُ	taran{u}	तरणु	swimming
تيرَ هَڻُ	teer{a} hanan{u}	तीर हणणु	archery
سُواري	suwaaree	सुवारी	riding
سِکِيو	sikhiyo	सिखियो	learnt
ننڍي	nandhe	नंढे	young
خُواري	khuwaaree	खुवारी	ill name

سَولو آيو،
سَولو وِيو

Sav{i}lo aayo, sav{i}lo viyo

सविलो आयो, सविलो वियो

Easy come, easy go.

سَولو	sav{i}lo	सविलो	easy
آيو	aayo	आयो	came
وِيو	viyo	वियो	go, went

عِشقُ ۽
کَستوُري ڳُجها
نَه رَهَنِ

Ishq{u} ai{n} khasturee gujhaa na rahan{i}

इश्कु ऐं ख़स्तूरी गुझा न रहनि

Love and fragrance cannot be hidden.

عِشقُ	ishq{u}	इश्कु	love, romance
کَستوُري	khasturee	खस्तूरी	musk, fragrance

وِيئِي ويلَ وَرانِي هَٿِ نَه اَچِي	Veyee vel[a] varaaye hath[i] na ache
	وेई वेल वराए हथि न अचे
	Lost time is never found.

وِيئِي	veyee	वेई	lost
ويلَ	vel[a]	वेल	time
وَرائِي	varaaye	वराए	again

نائِي بِنا نَرُ ويگانو	Naane binaa nar[u] vegaano
	नाणे बिना नरु वेगाणो
	A light purse makes a heavy heart.

نائِي	naane	नाणे	money
نَرُ	nar[u]	नरु	man
ويگانو	vegaano	वेगाणो	unhappy, distracted

ڏَڳا ڏُهَڻُ	Dhagaa duhan[u]
	ढगा डुहणु
	Like squeezing water out of a rock.

ڏَڳا	dhagaa	ढगा	bulls
ڏُهَڻُ	duhanu	डुहणु	to milk

روزي روٽِي يا نَصِيبُ	Rozee rotee yaa naseeb[u]
	रोज़ी रोटी या नसीबु
	To live from hand to mouth.

نَصِيبُ	naseeb[u]	नसीबु	fate

سُتا سوُرَ نَہ Sutaa soor[a] na jaagaai
جاڳاءِ सुता सूर न जाग़ाइ

Let sleeping dogs lie.

سُتا	sutaa	सुता	sleeping
سوُرَ	soor[a]	सूर	pain
جاڳاءِ	jaagaai	जाग़ाइ	awaken

جو نِمِيو، سو Jo nim[i]yo, so gauro
ڳورو जो निमियो, सो ग़ौरो

The lowest boughs bear the juiciest fruit.

| نِمِيو | nim[i]yo | निमियो | bow down |
| ڳورو | gauro | ग़ौरो | heaviest |

سُکُ ڏُکُ عُمِرِ Sukh[u] dukh[u] umir[i] jo taqaazo
جو تَقاضو सुखु दुखु उमिरि जो तक़ाज़ो

Joy and sorrow are the light and shade of life.

| عُمِرِ | umir[i] | उमिरि | age |
| تَقاضو | taqaazo | तक़ाज़ो | inevitability |

تُرتُ دانُ، مَها Turt[u] daan[u], mahaa puny[u]
پُڃُ तुर्तु दानु, महा पुञु

To give immediately is great charity.

تُرتُ	turt[u]	तुर्तु	instantly
دانُ	daan[u]	दानु	charity
مَها	mahaa	महा	great magnitude
پُڃُ	puny[u]	पुञु	good deed

کُتي جو پُڇُ نڙ ۾ ڀِه سِڌو نه ٿِيي

Kute jo puchhᵘ nadᵃ meiⁿ bi sidho na thiye

कुते जो पुछु नड़ में बि सिधो न थिए

A leopard never changes its spots.

کُتي	kute	कुते	dog
پُڇُ	puchhᵘ	पुछु	tail
نڙ	nadᵃ	नड़	pipe
سِڌو	sidho	सिधो	straight

ٻِني جو گَھرُ، هميشه ڊَرُ

B̲ie jo gharᵘ, hameshahᵃ darᵘ

बिए जो घरु, हमेशह डरु

A man's home is his castle.

ٻِني	b̲ie	बिए	others
گَھرُ	gharᵘ	घरु	house
ڊَرُ	darᵘ	डरु	fearful

ڪاٺي مانيءَ جي ڳَلَ نه لاهِه

Khaanee maaneeᵃ jee khalᵃ na laahⁱ

खाणी मानीᵃ जी खल न लाहि

Don't rob the poor.

ڪاٺي	khaanee	खाणी	burnt
مانيءَ	maaneeᵃ	मानीᵃ	Indian unleavened bread (chapati)
ڳَلَ	khalᵃ	खल	top layer

شاديءَ آهي
دهليءَ
جو لَڏُون
کاءُ تَہ بہ
پڇتاءِ، نَہ کاءُ
تَہ بہ پَڇتاءِ

Shaadee aahe dehlee[a] jo la<u>d</u>oo[n], khaau ta bi pachh'taai, na khaau ta bi pachh'taai

शादी आहे दिहलीअ जो लड्डूं खाउ त बि पछिताइ, न खाउ त बि पछिताइ

Marriage is like sweetmeat: you regret eating them, you regret not eating them.

شادي	shaadee	शादी	marriage
دِهلي	dehlee[a]	दिहली	Delhi
لَڏُون	la<u>d</u>oo[n]	लड्डूं	sweetmeat
کاءُ	khaau	खाउ	eat
پَڇتاءِ	pachh'taai	पछिताइ	repent
نَہ کاءُ	na khaau	न खाउ	do not eat

کَمُ ٿورو، قَرِ قَرِ گھڻي

Kam[u] thoro, phar[i]-phar[i] ghanee

कमु थोरो, फरि फरि घणी

More talk and less action.

کَمُ	kam[u]	कमु	work
ٿورو	thoro	थोरो	little
قَرِ قَرِ	phar[i]-phar[i]	फरिफरि	activity
گھڻي	ghanee	घणी	more

لُچائِي اَچي
پيرَنِ پَرِ، ۽
وَڃي گوڏَنِ پَرِ

Luchaaee ache peranⁱ bharⁱ, aiⁿ vanye go<u>d</u>anⁱ bharⁱ

लुचाई अचे पेरनि भरि, ऐं वञे गोड़नि भरि

Mischief comes by the pound and goes by the ounce.*

لُچائِي	luchaaee	लुचाई	mischief
پيرَنِ پَرِ	peranⁱ bharⁱ	पेरनि भरि	on feet
گوڏَنِ پَرِ	go<u>d</u>anⁱ bharⁱ	गोड़नि भरि	on knees

ٺاهِه، نَه تَه داهِه

Thaahⁱ, na ta daahⁱ

ठाहि, न त डाहि

Make or break.

ٺاهِه	thaahⁱ	ठाहि	make
داهِه	daahⁱ	डाहि	spoil

تيلِيءَ مان ٿَنڀُ

Teelee^a maaⁿ thambh^u

तीली^अ मां थंभु

Make a mountain out of a molehill.

تيلِيءَ	teelee^a	तीली	matchstick
ٿَنڀُ	thambh^u	थंभु	pillar, column

هَڙَ سَکڻِي، لوڎَ گھڻِي

Ha<u>d</u>^a sakhinee, lo<u>d</u>^a ghanee

हड़ सखिणी, लोड़ घणी

More poke† than pudding.‡

هَڙَ	ha<u>d</u>^a	हड़	bundle
لوڎَ	lo<u>d</u>^a	लोड़	movement

---

*Japanese proverb, †Bag, ‡1828

مَنگِيو نَه مائـِي،
لِکِيو مائـِي

Mang'yo na maane, likh'yo maane

मङियो न माणे, लिखियो माणे

Marriages are made in heaven.

مَنگِيو	mang'yo	मङियो	engagement
لِکِيو	likh'yo	लिखियो	destiny

سُکَنِ پُٽِيان
ڏُکَ، گھوڙِيا
سُکَ ڏُکَنِ رِيءَ

Sukhan' puth'yaaⁿ dukh^a, ghoriyaa sukh^a dukhan' ree^a

सुखनि पुठियां दुख, घोरिया सुख दुखनि रीअ

Misfortunes tell us what good fortune is.

سُکَ	sukh^a	सुख	happiness
ڏُکَ	dukh^a	दुख	sorrow
گھوڙِيا	ghoriyaa	घोरिया	sacrifice

قُرِّيءَ قُرِّيءَ
تَلاءُ

Phudee^a phudee^a talaau

फुड़ीअ फुड़ीअ तलाउ

Many a little makes a mickle.*

قُرِّيءَ	phudee^a	फुड़ीअ	drop
تَلاءُ	talaau	तलाउ	pond

---

*Plenty

هَڙ ۾ هَرِيڙُون، | Had[a] mein hareedoo[n], god[i] mein pataashaa
گوڈِ ۾ پَتاشا | हड़ में हरीड़ूं गोडि में पताशा

More show than substance.

هَڙ	had[a]	हड	bundle
هَرِيڙُون	hareedoo[n]	हरीड़ूं	dried dates
گوڈِ	god[i]	गोडि	lungi
پَتاشا	pataashaa	पताशा	aerated sugar discs

ڏُکُ ساٿِيءَ بِنا | <u>D</u>ukh[u] saathee[a] bina na ache
نَه اَچِي | ड़ुखु साथी[a] बिना न अचे

Misfortune never comes singly.

| ڏُکُ | <u>d</u>ukh[u] | ड़ुखु | sorrow |
| ساٿِي | saathee[a] | साथी | companion |

مُڙسَ جِي | Mud[u]s[a] jee kamaaee, zaal[a] jee sahed[a]
ڪَمائي، زالَ | मुड़ुस जी कमाई, ज़ाल जी सहेड़
جِي سَهيڙَ |

Men make wealth, women make homes.

مُڙسَ	mud[u]s[a]	मुड़ुस	husband
زالَ	zaal[a]	ज़ाल	wife
سَهيڙَ	sahed[a]	सहेड़	care

ٻِنِي جِي ڀيٽَ | <u>B</u>ie jee bhet[a] paan[a] saa[n] karan[u]
پاڻَ سان ڪَرَڻُ | बिए जी भेट पाण सां करणु

Measure everyone's corn by your own bushel.

| ٻِنِي | <u>b</u>ie | बिए | others |
| ڀيٽَ | bhet[a] | भेट | comparison |

عيسيٰ نَه موسىٰ، بَڙا پيرُ پَئسا

Eesaa na Moosaa, badaa peer^u paisaa

ईसा न मूसा, बड़ा पीरु पैसा

Money makes the mare go.

عيسيٰ موسىٰ	eesaa moosaa	ईसा–मूसा	Jesus and Moses
پيرُ	peer^u	पीरु	holy man
پَئسا	paisaa	पैसा	money

هُجيئي ناٹو، تَه گهُمُ لاڙِڪاڻو

Hujeyee naano, ta ghum^u Laadⁱkaano

हुजेई नाणो, त घुमु लाड़िकाणो

Money makes the mare go.

هُجيئي	hujeyee	हुजेई	if you have
ناٹو	naano	नाणो	money
گهُمُ	ghum^u	घुमु	tour
لاڙِڪاڻو	Laadⁱkaano	लाड़िकाणो	Larkana

جَهِڙو راجا، تَهِڙي پرِجا

Jehⁱdo raajaa, tehⁱdee prijaa

जहिड़ो राजा, तहिड़ी प्रजा

Muddy springs will have muddy streams.

جَهِڙو	jehⁱdo	जहिड़ो	like
راجا	raajaa	राजा	king
پرِجا	prijaa	प्रजा	subjects

نَه دَمُ، نَه بَمُ

Na dam^u, na bam^u

न दमु, न बमु

No guts, no glory.

دَمُ	dam^u	दमु	strength
بَمُ	bam^u	बमु	pride

Aaya Pir, Bhagga Mir and Other Sindhi Proverbs

أَنڌي جي جوءِ
جو واهي اَللهه

Andhe jee joi jo vaahee Alaah[u]

अंधे जी जोइ जो वाही अलाहु

The blind man's wife has no protector but God.

أَنڌي	andhe	अंधे	blind man
جوءِ	joi	जोइ	wife
واهي	vaahee	वाही	protector
اَللههُ	Alaah[u]	अलाहु	God

جَنهن تَنِ لاڳي،
سو تَنُ ڄاڻي

Jenh[in] tan[i] laagee, so tan[u] jaane

जंहिं तनि लागी, सो तनु जाणे

No one knows the weight of another's burden.

| تَنُ | tan[u] | तनु | body |

بي خَبَري
خُوش خَبَري

Be khabaree, khush khabaree

बे ख़बरी, ख़ुश ख़बरी

No news is good news.

بي	be	बे	without
خَبَري	khabaree	ख़बरी	news
خُوش	khush	ख़ुश	happy

نَنهَن سان
چِجي، تَہ
ڪاتي چو
هَٽِجي

Nanh[an] saa[n] chhije, ta kaatee chho han[i]je

नंहं सां छिजे, त काती छो हणिजे

Never draw your dirk when a dint will do.*

نَنهَن	nanh[an]	नंहं	nail
چِجي	chhije	छिज़े	tear
ڪاتي	kaatee	काती	sword

هِڪَ ماءُ ڊَهَہ،
بارَ ساندي
پَرَ ڊَهَہ بارَ
هِڪَ ماءُ نَہ
سَنڀاليِنِ

Hik[a] maa[u] dah[a] baar[a] saandhe, par[a] dah[a] baar[a] hik[a] maau na sambhaaleen[i]

हिक माउ ड॒ह बा॒र सांढे, पर ड॒ह बा॒र हिक माउ न संभालीनि

One mother can look after ten children but ten children cannot care for one mother.

ماءُ	maa[u]	माउ	mother
ساندي	saandhe	सांढे	protect
سَنڀاليِنِ	sambhaaleen[i]	संभालीनि	look after

مِروُنَنان مَوتُ،
مَلُوڪان
شِڪارُ

Miroo[n]aa[n] maut[u], malookaa[n] shikaar[u]

मिरूंआं मौतु, मलूकां शिकारु

One man's food is another man's poison.

مِروُنَنان	miroo[n]aa[n]	मिरूंआं	animals
مَلُوڪان	malookaa[n]	मलूकां	nobility
شِڪارُ	shikaar[u]	शिकारु	hunt

---

*Old English proverb

Aaya Pir, Bhagga Mir and Other Sindhi Proverbs • 159

اَکِ جو ڏِٺو
ڪَنَ جي ٻُڌَلَ
کان زوردارُ

Akh[i] jo ditho kan[a] je budhal[a] khaa[n] zordaar[u]

अखि जो डिठो कन जे बुधल खां ज़ोरदारु

One eyewitness is better than ten hearsayers.

اَکِ	akh[i]	अखि	eye
ڪَنَ	kan[a]	कन	ear
زوردارُ	zordaar[u]	ज़ोरदारु	weighty

هِڪُ ڪُوڙُ
ڍَڪَنَ لاءِ ڏَهَ
ڪُوڙُ ڳالهائِڻا
پَوَنِ

Hik[u] kood[u] dhakan[a] laai dah[a] kood[a] gaalhaainaa pavan[i]

हिकु कूड़ु ढकण लाइ डह कूड़ ग़ाल्हाइणा पवनि

One lie needs seven to wait upon it.

ڪُوڙُ	kood[u]	कूड़ु	lie
ڍَڪَنَ	dhakan[a]	ढकण	cover
ڳالهائِڻا	gaalhaainaa	ग़ाल्हाइणा	to
پَوَنِ		पवनि	speak

کاڌي کان ڏِٺو
ڀَلو

Khaadhe khaa[n] ditho bhalo

खाधे खां डिठो भलो

Some things are better seen rather than experienced.

کاڌي	khaadhe	खाधे	eat
ڏِٺو	ditho	डिठो	to see
ڀَلو	bhalo	भलो	better

ڪَٿو ڪَٿو   Kano kano jholo bhare
جھولو يَري   कणो कणो झोलो भरे

One grain fills not a sack but helps its fellows.

ڪَٿو	kano	कणो	grain
جھولو	jholo	झोलो	cloth bag
يَري	bhare	भरे	fills

اُدَمَ کان سَواءِ   Udam^a khaa^n sawaai bhaag^u bi mando
ڀاڳُ ڀِه مَندو   उदम खां सवाइ भागु बि मंदो

Ossing comes to bossing.*

اُدَمَ	udam^a	उदम	effort
ڀاڳُ	bhaag^u	भागु	destiny
مَندو	mando	मंदो	dull

غَرِيبَ جِي   Gareeb^a jee joi, sabh^inee jee bhaajaaee
جوءِ، سَڀِني   ग़रीब जी जोइ, सभिनी जी भाजाई
جي ڀاڄائي

Poor relations talk of high connections.

غَرِيبَ	gareeb^a	ग़रीब	poor man
جوءِ	joi	जोइ	wife
ڀاڄائي	bhaajaaee	भाजाई	sister-in-law

---

*Cheshire proverb, 15th century

چَئِين آني جي چَٽي، بارهين آني جي پَٽي

Chaee[n] aane jee chatee, <u>b</u>aarhe[n] aane jee patee

चई आने जी चटी, बारहें आने जी पटी

Prevention is better than cure.

چَئِين آني	chaee[n] aane	चई आने	four annas
بارهين آني	<u>b</u>aarhe[n] aane	बारहें आने	twelve annas
پَٽي	patee	पटी	bandage

لَڇمي ويئي، تَه لَڇَڻ ڀه ويا

Lachh[a]mee veyee, ta lachhan[a] bi viyaa

लछमी वेई, त लछण बि विया

Poverty is an enemy to good manners.

| لَڇمي | Lachh[a]mee | लछमी | wealth |
| لَڇَڻ | lachhan[a] | लछण | virtues |

کاڌي مُکياري

Khaadhe mukhyaaree

खाधे मुखयारी

The proof of the pudding is in the eating.

| کاڌي | khaadhe | खाधे | eat |
| مُکياري | mukhyaaree | मुख्यारी | approval |

پَئسي پَلو مَهانگو، رُپَئي پَلو سَهانگو

Paise pallo mahaango, rupae pallo sahaango

पैसे पलो महांगो, रुपए पलो सहांगो

Over time, things become expensive.

پَلو	pallo	पलो	river fish
مَهانگو	mahaango	महांगो	expensive
پَئسي	paise	पैसे	$1/64$ of a rupee
سَهانگو	sahaango	सहांगो	inexpensive

پَرَٽُ چَوي
ڏُونگھي کي،
هَلُ ڙي نَہ
ٽونگا

Paran[u] chave doonghe khe, hal[u] re ti-toonga

परणु चवे डूंघे खे, हलु ड़े टि टूंगा

The pot calling the kettle black.

پَرَٽُ	paran[u]	परण	sieve
ڏُونگھي	doonghe	डूंघे	coconut shell
ٽَہ ٽونگا	ti-toonga	टि टूंगा	three-holed one

اُڀَ م جِنِ جُون
اَکِڙِيُون
پَلئَہ تِنِ کي
ککِڙِيُون

Ubh[a] mei[n] jin[i] joo[n] akh[i]diyoon, palai tin[i] khe khakh[i]diyoon

उभ में जिनि जूं अखिड़ियूं पलइ तिनि खे खखिड़ियूं

Pride goes before a fall.

اُڀَ	ubh[a]	उभ	sky
اَکِڙِيُون	akh[i]diyoon	अखिड़ियूं	eyes
پَلئَہ	palai	पलइ	get
ککِڙِيُون	khakh[i]diyoon	खखिड़ियूं	stones

اَنڌي اَڳِيان
آرِسي

Andhe ag[i]yaa[n] aar[i]see

अंधे अगियां आरिसी

A blind man under a lamp post.

اَنڌي	andhe	अंधे	blind
اَڳِيان	ag[i]yaa[n]	अगियां	in front of
آرِسي	aar[i]see	आरिसी	mirror

ذَنَ جو ذَكِيَلُ
بي ڊوهي

Dhan[a] jo dhak[i]yal[u] be-dohee
धन जो ढकियलु बेडोही
The rich have no faults.

ذَنَ	dhan[a]	धन	wealth
ذَكِيَلُ	dhak[i]yal[u]	ढकियलु	covered
بيڊوهي	be-dohee	बेडोही	faultless

شاهوڪارُ
ڪائي ذَنَ،
غَرِيبُ ڪائي اَنُ

Shaahookaar[u] khaaye dhan[u], gareeb[u] khaaye an[u]
शाहूकारु खाए धनु, ग़रीबु खाए अनु
The rich eat money but the poor eat food.

شاهوڪارُ	shaahookaar[u]	शाहूकारु	wealthy
غَرِيبُ	gareeb[u]	ग़रीबु	poor
اَنُ	an[u]	अनु	grain

سُورَ پي وَڄُّ

Soor[a] pee vanyan[u]
सूर पी वञणु
To swallow a bitter pill.

آئيءَ ويلَ ڪَمُ اَچي

Aaee[a] vel[a] kam[u] ache
आईअ वेल कमु अचे
To save for a rainy day.

Hath[u] na kar[i] et[i]ro, hath[a] vinyaayaa veer[a], kiree p[i]yaa ket[i]raa, maad[i]yun[i] mathaa[n] meer

हठु न करि एतिरो, हठ विञाया वीर
किरी पिया केतिरा, माड़ियुनि मथां मीर

Be wise; soar not too high to fall, but stoop to rise.

	hath[a]	हठु	pride
	veer[a]	वीर	courageous
	meer	मीर	aristocracy

Zibaan[a] jo nik[i]tal[u] andar[i] na varando

ज़िबान जो निकितलु अंदरि न वरंदो

Words spoken cannot be taken back.

| | zibaan[a] | ज़िबान | tongue |
| | varando | वरंदो | return |

Aar[i] yaa paar[i]

आरि या पारि

Shape up or ship out.

Puth[i] varaae ke[n]h[in] na dithee

पुठि वराए कंहिं न डिठी

It's easy to see the faults of others, but difficult to see one's own.

| | puth[i] | पुठि | back |
| | varaae | वराए | turn |

بُڏُ يا تَرُ

B^ud^u yaa tar^u

बुडु या तरु

Sink or swim.

| بُڏُ | b^ud^u | बुडु | drown |
| تَرُ | tar^u | तरु | swim |

چُلهه ويني، دِلِ ويني

Chulhⁱ veyee, dilⁱ veyee

चुल्हि वेई, दिलि वेई

Separate hearths make separate hearts.

چُلهه	chulhⁱ	चुल्हि	hearth
دِلِ	dilⁱ	दिलि	heart
ويني	veyee	वेई	lost

وَنڊِ ورهاءِ، سُکُ پاءِ

Vandhⁱ virhaai, sukh^u paai

वंढि विरहाइ, सुखु पाइ

Share and share alike.

| وَنڊِ | vandhⁱ | वंढि | distribute |

خَرچُ کاءُ، ڏِني اَللهه

Kharch^u khaa^u, diye Alaah^u

ख़र्चु खाउ, ड़िए अलाहु

Give and spend and God will send.

| خَرچُ | kharch^u | ख़र्चु | spend |
| اَللهه | Alaah^u | अलाहु | God |

کوئلنِ جي
دلاليءَ مَ
هَٿُ بہ ڪارو،
مُنهن بہ ڪارو

Koilan[i] jee dalaalee[a] mein,
hath[u] bi kaaro, munh[un] bi kaaro
कोइलनि जी दलाली[a] में, हथु बि कारो, मुंहं बि कारो
The smith and his penny both are black.

کوئلنِ	koilan[i]	कोइलनि	coals
دَلالي	dalaalee[a]	दलाली	trade
ڪارو	kaaro	कारो	black

مَرضُ پُڇي نَہ اچي

Marz[u] puchhee na ache
मर्जु पुछी न अचे
Sickness always comes unannounced.

| مَرضُ | marz[u] | मर्जु | illness |
| پُڇي | puchhee | पुछी | ask |

مَرضُ اچي
گھوڙي تي،
ءِ وَڃي جوُن
وانگُرُ

Marz[u] ache ghode te, ai[n] vanye joo[n] vaangur[u]
मर्जु अचे घोड़े ते, ऐं वञे जूं वांगुरु
Sickness comes on horseback but departs on foot.

مَرضُ	marz[u]	मर्जु	sickness
گھوڙي	ghode	घोड़े	horse
جوُن	joo[n]	जूं	lice

بارُ اَکِ کان
ٻاهرِ ٿِيو تَہ
ڪَرِيو

Baar[u] akh[i] khaa[n] baahir[i] th[i]yo ta khar[i]yo
बारु अखि खां बाहिरि थियो त खरियो
Children are spoiled by being ignored.

بارُ	baar[u]	बारु	child
اَکِ	akh[i]	अखि	eye
ڪَرِيو	khar[i]yo	खरियो	spoiled

Aaya Pir, Bhagga Mir and Other Sindhi Proverbs • 167

مينهن پَنهنجي كاراڻ نه ڏِسي

Menh[in] pe[n]hinjee kaaraan[i] na d̲ise

मेंहिं पंहिंजी काराणि न ड़िसे

Sweep before your own door.

| مينهن | menh[in] | मेंहिं | buffalo |
| كاراڻ | kaaraan[i] | काराणि | blackness |

چورَنِ مَتَّان مورَ

Choran[i] mathaa[n] mor[a]

चोरनि मथां मोर

Set a thief to catch a thief.

چورَنِ	choran[i]	चोरनि	thief
مَتَّان	mathaa[n]	मथां	above
مورَ	mor[a]	मोर	peacock

دیرِ آیا، دُرُستُ آیا

Der[i] aaya, durust[u] aayaa

देरि आया, दुरुस्तु आया

Better late than never.

| دیرِ | der[i] | देरि | late |
| دُرُستُ | durust[u] | दुरुस्तु | correct |

هَٿَ ۾ قُرانُ، ڪَڇَ ۾ ڇُري

Hath[a] mei[n] Quraan[u], kachh[a] mei[n] chhuree

हथ में कुरानु, कछ में छुरी

Shake your hand and stab you in the back.*

هَٿَ	hath[a]	हथ	hand
قُرانُ	Quraan[u]	कुरानु	Quran
ڪَڇَ	kachh[a]	कछ	armpit
ڇُري	chhuree	छुरी	knife

---

*Afghani proverb

Ghar^a khe baahⁱ lagan^a mehil^a khooh^u khot'je

घर खे बाहि लगण महिल खूहु खोटिजे

Start digging a well when the house is on fire.

	baahⁱ	बाहि	fire
	khooh^u	खूह	well
	khot'je	खोटिजे	dig

Jo na kuchhe, uho ghano kuchhe

जो न कुछे, उहो घणो कुछे

Silence is the unbearable repartee.

	kuchhe	कुछे	speak
	ghano	घणो	a lot

Paanee^a mathaaⁿ jhoop'daa, mur'kh^a unya maranⁱ

पाणी^अ मथां झूपिड़ा, मूरिख उञ मरनि

The foolish live on the riverbank but die of thirst.

	jhoop'daa	झूपिड़ा	huts
	mur'kh^a	मूरिख	foolish
	unya	उञ	thirst

دوستَ ڏانهُن
هَٿُ ڊِگھيرَٽُ
سَوِلي ڳالھہ

Dost^a <u>d</u>aanh^{un} hath^u digheran^u savⁱlee gaalhⁱ

दोस्त ड़ांहुं हथु डिघेरणु सविली ग़ाल्हि

The road to a friend's house is never long.

دوستَ	dost^a	दोस्त	friend
ڊِگھيرَٽُ	digheran^u	डिघेरणु	stretch
سَوِلي	savⁱlee	सविली	easy

جو رَبَ کي
پيارو، سو سَڀَ
کي پيارو

Jo Rab^a khe pⁱyaaro, so sabh^a khe pⁱyaaro

जो रब खे पियारो, सो सभ खे पियारो

Those whom the Gods love, are loved by everyone.*

رَبَ	Rab^a	रब	God
پيارو	pⁱyaaro	पियारो	beloved
سَڀَ	sabh^a	सभ	everyone

بَصَرُ يَڃَٽُ کان
سَواءِ بانسَ نَہ
نِڪِرَندي

Basar^u bhunyana khaaⁿ savaai baaⁿs^a na nikⁱrandee

बसरु भुञणु खां सवाइ बांस न निकिरंदी

You can't make an omelette without breaking eggs.

بَصَرُ	basar^u	बसरु	onion
يَڃَٽُ	bhunyana	भुञणु	sauté
بانسَ	baaⁿs^a	बांस	smell

---

*Punjabi proverb

مَڇِيءَ مان
ڪَنڊا ڪَڍَڻُ

Machhee[a] maa[n] kandaa kadhan[u]

मछी[अ] मां कंडा कढणु

To split hairs.

مَڇِيءَ	machhee[a]	मछी[अ]	fish
ڪَنڊا	kandaa	कंडा	bones
ڪَڍَڻُ	kadhan[u]	कढणु	remove

گھَڻِي زالين
گھَرُ نَه هَلي
گھَڻي مَردين
هَرُ نَه هَلي

Ghane[n] zaale[n] ghar[u] na hale, ghane[n] marde[n] har[u] na hale

घणे ज़ालें घरु न हले, घणे मरदें हरु न हले

Too many cooks spoil the broth.

زالين	zaale[n]	ज़ालें	women
گھَرُ	ghar[u]	घरु	household
مَردين	marde[n]	मरदें	men
هَرُ	har[u]	हरु	plough

گَنڊُ گَنڊَ سان نَه
صَفا ٿِئي

Gand[u] gand[a] saa[n] na safaa thiye

गंदु गंद सां न सफ़ा थिए

Two wrongs do not make a right.

گَنڊَ	gand[a]	गंदु	dirt
صَفا	safaa	सफ़ा	clean

جيسين ساسُ،
تيسين آسَ

Jeseen saas[u], teseen aas[a]

जेसीं सासु, तेसीं आस

While there is life, there is hope.

ساسُ	saas[u]	सासु	breath
آسَ	aas[a]	आस	hope

گِدَڙُ ڊاکَ نَه پُڄي، آکي ٿُو کَٽا

Gidadᵘ daakhᵃ na puje, aakhe thoo khataa

गिदड़ु डाख न पुजे, आखे थू खटा

The grapes are sour.

پُڄي	puje	पुजे	reach
آکي	aakhe	आखे	say
کَٽا	khataa	खटा	sour

ڳالهه مان ڳالهوڙو

Gaalhⁱ maaⁿ gaalhodo

गाल्हि मां गाल्होड़ो

Storm in a teacup.

| ڳالهه | gaalhⁱ | गाल्हि | friendly talk |
| ڳالهوڙو | gaalhodo | गाल्होड़ो | quarrel |

جتي لڳي باهِه، اُتي اَڄي سيڪُ

Jite lage baahⁱ, ute ache sekᵘ

जिते लगे बाहि, उते अचे सेकु

The wearer knows where the shoe pinches.

| باهِه | baahⁱ | बाहि | fire |
| سيڪُ | sekᵘ | सेकु | scorch |

جَهڙو لڳي واءُ، تَهڙي ڏِجي پُٺِ

Jehⁱdo lage waau, tehⁱdee dije puthⁱ

जहिड़ो लगे वाउ, तहिड़ी डिजे पुठि

Go where the wind blows.

| واءُ | waau | वाउ | wind |
| پُٺِ | puthⁱ | पुठि | back |

| جو نِمِيو، سو جُرِّيو | Jo nim'yo, so jud'yo |

जो निमियो, सो जुड़ियो

The boughs that bear the most hang the lowest.

| نِمِيو | nim'yo | निमियो | bows |
| جُرِّيو | jud'yo | जुड़ियो | raised |

| يا اَڏِ يا چَڏِ | Yaa ad', yaa chhad' |

या अडि या छडि

Time to fish or cut the bait.

| اَڏِ | ad' | अडि | build |
| چَڏِ | chhad' | छडि | leave |

| ڦاٽِڙِي نَه سِبي، سا راجا جي نَه راڻي | Phaat'dee na sibe, saa raajaa jee na raanee |

फाटिड़ी न सिबे, सा राजा जी न राणी

Master yourself, and become king of the world around you.

| ڦاٽِڙِي | phaat'dee | फाटिड़ी | tear |
| سِبي | sibe | सिबे | mend |

| پَنَّ ويڻي، تَه گھُونگھَٽُ ڪيها | Pinanᵃ vethee, ta ghoonghatᵘ kehaa |

पिनन वेठी, त घूंघटु केहा

There is no stripping a naked man.

| پَنَّ | pinanᵃ | पिनन | beg |
| گھُونگھَٽُ | ghoonghatᵘ | घूंघटु | veil |

جي گُڙ سان | Je gudᵃ saaⁿ mare, ta zehirᵘ chho dije
مَري، تَه زَهِرُ | जे गुड़ सां मरे, त ज़हिरु छो ड़िजे
چو ڏِجي | **Take not a musket to kill a butterfly.**

پائيءَ پائيءَ | Paaeeᵃ paaeeᵃ paiso thaahⁱyo, paise thaahⁱyo rupayo
پئسو ٿاهِيو | पाईअ पाईअ पैसो ठाहियो, पैसे ठाहियो रुपयो
پئسي ٿاهِيو رُپَيو | **Take care of the pennies and the pounds will take care of themselves.***

سَچُ تَه بيٺو نَچُ | Sachᵘ ta beetho nachᵘ
| सचु त बीठो नचु
| **Truth will triumph.**

| سَچُ | sachᵘ | सचु | truth |
| نَچُ | nachᵘ | नचु | dance |

---

*Note:

4 cowrie shells	=	1 paaee
3 paaee	=	1 paisa
4 paise	=	1 anna
16 annas	=	1 rupee
100 paise	=	1 rupee

رَدِي پَڪِي يا نَصِيبُ

Radhee pakee yaa naseeb[u]

रधी पकी या नसीबु

There's many a slip between the cup and the lip.

رَدِي پَڪِي	radhee pakee	रधी पकी	cooked meal
نَصِيبُ	naseeb[u]	नसीबु	fortune

تِرَ تان ڳُٽِي، سَوَ چوٽُون کائي

Tir[a] taa[n] guthee, sav[a] chotoo[n] khaae

तिर तां गुथी, सव चोटूं खाए

There's many a slip between the cup and the lip.

تِرَ	tir[a]	तिर	hair's breadth
ڳُٽِي	guthee	गुथी	miss
چوٽُون	chotoo[n]	चोटूं	injuries

وَقتَ کي آهي ويسَرِ

Vaqt[a] khe aahe vesar[i]

वक़्त खे आहे वेसरि

Time is a great healer.

وَقتَ	vaqt[a]	वक़्त	time
ويسَرِ	vesar[i]	वेसरि	forgetting

جو مُڙِيو، سو جُڙِيو

Jo mud[i]yo, so jud[i]yo

जो मुड़ियो, सो जुड़ियो

The more noble, the more humble.

مُڙِيو	mud[i]yo	मुड़ियो	accept defeat
جُڙِيو	jud[i]yo	जुड़ियो	won

Aaya Pir, Bhagga Mir and Other Sindhi Proverbs • 175

بَه ڀائُرَ، تِيُون ليکو

<u>B</u>a bhaaur[a], t'yo[n] lekho

ब़ भाउर, टियों लेखो

Though they are brothers, their pockets are not sisters.

ڀائُرَ	bhaaur[a]	भाउर	brothers
ليکو	lekho	लेखो	accounts

ڪارو ويو
ڪَمِري وَٽِ،
رَنگُ نَه مَٽائي،
پَرَ عادَتَ
ضرُورُ مَٽائي

Kaaro v'yo kam're vat[i], rang[u] na mataae, par[a] aadat[a] zaroor matae

कारो वियो कमिरे वटि, रंगु न मटाए, पर आदत ज़रूर मटाए

The fox changes not its skin but its habits.

ڪارو	kaaro	कारो	black
ڪَمِري	kam're	कमिरे	less black
مَٽائي	mataae	मटाए	change
عادَتَ	aadat[a]	आदत	habit

ٻِئي جي ڪَمَ ۾ ٽَنگَ اَڙائڻُ

<u>B</u>ie je kam[a] mei[n] tang[a] adaain[u]

ब़िए जे कम में टंग अड़ाइणु

To put a spoke in someone's wheel.

ٽَنگَ	tang[a]	टंग	leg
اَڙائڻُ	adaain[u]	अड़ाइणु	to hinder

ڪَبابَ ۾ هَڏِي

Kabaab mei[n] ha<u>d</u>ee

कबाब में हड़ी

Two's company, three's a crowd.

هَڏِي	ha<u>d</u>ee	हड़ी	bone

جِنَنْ ٿَڌِ، تِنَنْ وَڌِ

Jeea^n thadh^i, teea^n wadh^i

जिअं थधि, तिअं वधि

To mend as sour ale mends in summer.

| ٿَڌِ | thadh^i | थधि | cold |
| وَڌِ | wadh^i | वधि | excess |

پَيسو هَرِ زِبانَ جاڻي

Paiso har^i zibaan^a jaane

पैसो हरि ज़िबान जाणे

A golden key opens any door.

پَيسو	paiso	पैसो	money
زِبانَ	zibaan^a	ज़िबान	language
جاڻي	jaane	जाणे	knows

واڻِيا بِه ڪُوڙا، واڻِيَنِ جا وَٽَ بِه ڪُوڙا

Vaaniyaa bi koodaa, vaaniyan^i jaa vat^a bi koodaa

वाणिया बि कूड़ा, वाणियनि जा वट बि कूड़ा

No deceit, no merchant.*

واڻِيا	vaaniyaa	वाणिया	tradesmen
وَٽَ	vat^a	वट	weights and measures
ڪُوڙا	koodaa	कूड़ा	false

جَنسي ڪو تَنسا مِلا

Jaise ko taisaa milaa

जैसे को तैसा मिला

Two knaves well met.[†]

---

*Afghan proverb, †Mathura proverb

جو چُلھہ تي،
سو دِلِ تي

Jo chulh[i] te, so dil[i] te
जो चुल्हि ते, सो दिलि ते
The family that eats together stays together.

| چُلھہ | chulh[i] | चुल्हि | hearth |
| دِلِ | dil[i] | दिलि | heart |

چورَنِ جا ڀاءُرَ
گنڊيچور

Choran[i] jaa bhaaur[a] gandheechor[a]
चोरनि जा भाउर गंढीचोर
They agree like pickpockets at a fair.

| گنڊيچور | gandheechor[a] | गंढीचोर | two of a kind |

بَہ شينِھَنَ ھِڪَ
ٻيلي ۾ نَہ ماپَنِ

Ba sheenh[an] hik[a] bele mei[n] na maapan[i]
ब शींहं हिक बेले में न मापनि
Two lions cannot rule in the same kingdom.

| شينِھَنَ | sheenh[an] | शींह | lions |
| ٻيلي | bele | बेले | forest |

بَہ تَرارُون
ھِڪَ مِيانَ ۾ نَہ ماپَنِ

Ba taraaroo[n] hik[a] miyaan[a] mei[n] na maapan[i]
ब तरारूं हिक मियाण में न मापनि
Two kings in one kingdom do not agree well together.

| تَرارُون | taraaroo[n] | तरारूं | swords |
| مِيانَ | miyaan[a] | मियाण | scabbard |

مورُ گھڻو ئي موچارو، پَرَ مورَ جا پيرَ ڏِنگا

Mor[u] ghano ee mochaaro, para mora jaa pera <u>d</u>ingaa

मोरु घणोई मोचारो, पर मोर जा पेर ड़िंगा

The peacock has fair feathers but foul feet.

موچارو	mochaaro	मोचारो	good-looking
ڏِنگا	<u>d</u>ingaa	ड़िंगा	crooked

سِرُ سَلامَتِ، تَہ پَڳڙِيُون ھَزار

Sir[u] salaamat[i], ta pag[i]d[i]yoo[n] hazaar[a]

सिरु सलामति, त पगिड़ियूं हज़ार

Where there is life, there is hope.*

سَلامَتِ	salaamat[i]	सलामति	intact
پَڳڙِيُون	pag[i]d[i]yoo[n]	पगिड़ियूं	turbans

مُٺِ تَہ مُڪَ، نَہ تَہ چُڪَ

Muth[i] ta muk[a], na ta chuk[a]

मुठि त मुक, न त चुक

United we stand, divided we fall.

مُٺِ	muth[i]	मुठि	fist
مُڪَ	muk[a]	मुक	hit
چُڪَ	chuk[a]	चुक	mistake

کُٿي ڏاڙھي ھَٿِ نَہ اَچي

Khuthee <u>d</u>aadhee hath[i] na ache

खुथी ड़ाढ़ी हथि न अचे

Time and tide wait for none.

کُٿي	khuthee	खुथी	thinning
ڏاڙھي	<u>d</u>aadhee	ड़ाढ़ी	beard

---

*Punjabi proverb

سُکَنِ گڏُ آلا

Sukan[i] ga_d_u aalaa

सुकनि गडु आला

To take the rough with the smooth.

| سُکَنِ | sukan[i] | सुकनि | dry |
| آلا | aalaa | आला | wet |

هِكُ تِيرُ، بَه شِكارَ

Hik[u] teer[u], _b_a shikaar[a]

हिकु तीरु, ब शिकार

Kill two birds with one stone.

| تِيرُ | teer[u] | तीरु | arrow |
| شِكارَ | shikaar[a] | शिकार | prey |

کيتي سِرَ سيتي

Khetee sir[a] setee

खेती सिर सेती

The footsteps of the farmer are his best fertilizer.

| کيتي | khetee | खेती | farming |
| سيتي | setee | सेती | oneself |

گُذِرِيَلَ گهڙي هَڊِ حاصِلُ نَه ٿِي

Guz[i]r[i]yal[a] ghadee had[i] haasil[u] na thie

गुज़िरियल घड़ी हडि हासिलु न थिए

Time and tide wait for none.

| گُذِرِيَلَ | guz[i]r[i]yal[a] | गुज़िरियल | past |
| گهڙي | ghadee | घड़ी | moment |

نیڪِي اَورُ
پُوچھ پُوچھ

Nekee aur poochh poochh

नेकी और पूछ पूछ

Take the goods that God gives.*

| نیڪِي | nekee | नेकी | good deed |
| پُوچھ | poochh | पूछ | question |

ڏِنِي مَکِ ڳِيھَنؙ ڏُکِي

<u>D</u>ithee makhⁱ geehan^u <u>d</u>ukhee

डिठी मखि गीहणु डुखी

What the eye doesn't see, the heart doesn't grieve over.

ڏِنِي	<u>d</u>ithee	डिठी	seen
مَکِ	makhⁱ	मखि	fly
ڳِيھَنؙ	geehan^u	गीहणु	swallow
ڏُکِي	<u>d</u>ukhee	डुखी	difficult

دُوڌِ ڪا دُوڌِ، پاڻي ڪا پاڻي

Doodhⁱ kaa doodhⁱ, paanee kaa paanee

दूधि का दूधि, पानी का पानी

Water and oil do not mix together.†

جھَجھِي ھُوند، جھَجھو فِڪُرُ

Jhajhee hoondⁱ, jhajho fikur^u

झझी हूंदि, झझो फ़िकुरु

Uneasy lies the head that wears a crown.

جھَجھِي	jhajhee	झझी	plenty
ھُوند	hoondⁱ	हूंदि	prosperity
فِڪُرُ	fikur^u	फ़िकुरु	anxiety

---

*Japanese proverb, †Rajasthani proverb

سُنيِ سوري   Suee sore dhaage khe
ڏاڳي کي   सुई सोरे धागे खे
                   Where the needle goes, the thread follows.

سُنيِ	suee	सुई	needle
سوري	sore	सोरे	pull, drag

ڀتِيُنِ کي بہ   Bhit'yun' khe bi kan^a aahin'
ڪَنَ آهِنِ   भितियुनि खे बि कन आहिनि
                   Walls have ears.

ڀتِيُنِ	bhi'iyun'	भितियुनि	walls
ڪَنَ	kan^a	कन	ears

جَهڙو ديسُ،   Jeh'do des^u, teh'do ves^u
تَهڙو ويسُ   जहिड़ो देसु, तहिड़ो वेसु
                   When in Rome, do as the Romans do.

ديسُ	des^u	देसु	country
ويسُ	ves^u	वेसु	dress

هِينَڙا گهُرُ، تَہ   Hee^{n}adaa ghur^u, ta ghurai^n
گهُرانءِ   हींअड़ा घुरु, त घुरांइ
                   You scratch my back, I scratch yours.

هِينَڙا	hee^{n}adaa	हींअड़ा	dear
گهُرُ	ghur^u	घुरु	love me
گهُرانءِ	ghurai^n	घुरांइ	love you back

لِکِھیو لوحُ نَہ مِٹِجي

Likh[i]yo loh[u] na mit[i]je

लिखियो लोहु न मिटिजे

Hanging and wiving goes by destiny.

لِکِھیو لوحُ	likh[i]yo	लिखियो	destiny
مِٹِجي	mit[i]je	मिटिजे	change

تَرارَ جو گھاءُ وِسِري، پَرَ زِبانَ جو گھاءُ نَہ وِسِري

Taraar[a] jo ghaau vis[i]re, par[a] zibaan[a] jo ghaau na vis[i]re

तरार जो घाउ विसिरे, पर ज़िबान जो घाउ न विसिरे

Words cut deeper than a knife.

تَرار	taraar[a]	तरार	sword
گھاءُ	ghaau	घाउ	wound
وِسِري	vis[i]re	विसिरे	forget
زِبان	zibaan[a]	ज़िबान	tongue

جَنہِن دَردَ جو داروُن ناهي سو مِٹھو ڪَري مَڃِجي

Jenh[in] dard[a] jo daaroo[n] naahe, so mitho kare many[i]je

जंहि दर्द जो दारूं नाहे, सो मिठो करे मञिजे

What cannot be cured must be endured.

دَردَ	dard[a]	दर्द	pain
داروُن	daaroo[n]	दारूं	medicine
ناهي	naahe	नाहे	none
مَڃِجي	many[i]je	मञिजे	accept

كَمَ پِي، كَلَ پَوِي

Kam{a} pie, kal{a} pave

कम पिए, कल पवे

The wearer knows where the shoe pinches.

| كَمَ | kam{a} | कम | work |
| كَلَ | kal{a} | कल | awareness |

تُنھنجو سو مُنھنجو،
مُنھنجي کي ھَٿُ نَہ لاءِ

Tu{n}hinjo so mu{n}hinjo, mu{n}hinje khe hath{u} na laai

तुहिंजो सो मुहिंजो, मुहिंजे खे हथु न लाइ

What's yours is mine and what's mine is my own.

تُنھنجو	tu{n}hinjo	तुहिंजो	yours
مُنھنجو	mu{n}hinjo	मुहिंजो	mine
ھَٿُ نَہ لاءِ	hath{u} na laai	हथु न लाइ	do not touch

ڏَندَ ھُئا تَہ
حَلوو نَہ ھو،
حَلوو آھي تَہ
ڏَندَ ناھِنِ

<u>D</u>and{a} huaa ta hal{i}vo na ho, hal{i}vo aahe ta <u>d</u>and{a} naahin{i}

ड़ंद हुआ त हलिवो न हो, हलिवो आहे त ड़ंद नाहिनि

When I find a dog, the stone cannot be found, when I find a stone, the dog cannot be found.

| ڏَندَ | <u>d</u>and{a} | ड़ंद | teeth |
| حَلوو | hal{i}vo | हलिवो | toffee |

قَرضي آهي Qarzee aahe marzee
مَرضي
कर्ज़ी आहे मर्ज़ी

Who goeth a-borrowing, goeth a-sorrowing.

| قَرضي | qarzee | कर्ज़ी | debtor |
| مَرضي | marzee | मर्ज़ी | sick person, patient |

گھوڙا ڏي گھوڙا Ghodaa de ghodaa
घोड़ा डे घोड़ा

Mayday, mayday.*

پَئسي بِنا پِيري، Paise binaa peeree, kare sabh^a jee khuwaree
ڪَري سَڀَ
جي خُواري
पैसे बिना पीरी, करे सभ जी खुवारी

When you have silver in your hair, you should have gold in your pockets.

پَئسي بِنا	paise binaa	पैसे बिना	without money
پِيري	peeree	पीरी	old age
خُواري	khuwaree	खुवारी	defame

مَساڻي گِيانُ Masaanee g^iyaan^u
मसाणी ज्ञानु

Bookish knowledge.

| مَساڻي | masaanee | मसाणी | crematorium |
| گِيانُ | g^iyaan^u | ज्ञानु | knowledge |

---

*In ancient times, villages had no police protection, and dacoits would loot the people. So, when the sound of hoofbeats was heard, the villagers would raise a cry of 'Horses! Horses!' so that everyone could rush home and lock their doors.

Aaya Pir, Bhagga Mir and Other Sindhi Proverbs

جَنھنکي اِيشورُ رَکي، تَنھنکي ڪيرُ چَکي	Jenhⁱⁿ khe Ishwar^u rakhe, tenhⁱⁿ khe ker^u chakhe जंहिंखे ईश्वरु रखे, तंहिंखे केरु चखे **Where God helps, nought can harm.** چَکي chakhe चखे harm
مارَنَ واري کان بَچائنَ وارو وڏو	Maaran^a vaare khaaⁿ bachaain^a waaro va<u>d</u>o मारण वारे खां बचाइण वारो वड़ो **The one who saves is greater than the one who kills.** بَچائنَ وارو bachaain^a waaro बचाइण वारो saviour
راڪي رامُ، تو ماري ڪَون	Raakhe Ram^u, to maare kaun राखे रामु, तो मारे कौन **What God wills, no frost can kill.** رامُ Ram^u रामु Ram
حَشَرُ چو مَتو آھي؟	Hashar^u chho mato aahe? हशरु छो मतो आहे? **Whose mare is dead?** حَشَرُ hashar^u हशरु lamentation

Nachan[a] vethee, ta ghoonghat[u] kehaa[n]

नचण वेठी, त घूंघटु केहां

Where the heart is past hope, the face is past shame.*

	nachan[a]	नचण	dance
	ghoonghat[u]	घूंघटु	veil
	kehaa[n]	केहां	redundant

Chaa[n]hee[na] kaatee[a] khe lage, yaa kaatee chaa[n]hee[na] khe, nuksaan[u] chaa[n]hee[na] jo

छांहीं कातीअ खे लगे, या काती छांहींअ खे, नुक़्सानु छांहींअ जो

Whether the pitcher strikes the stone, or the stone the pitcher, it is bad for the pitcher.

	chaa[n]hee[na]	छांहीं	watermelon
	kaatee	काती	sword
	nuksaan[u]	नुक़्सानु	damage

Man[u] aahe, ta manzil[i] aahe

मनु आहे, त मंज़िलि आहे

Where there is a will, there is a way.

	man[u]	मनु	determination
	manzil[i]	मंज़िलि	goal

---

*Japanese proverb

جِتي چاهَه، اُتي راهَه

Jite chaah[a], ute raah[a]

जिते चाह, उते राह

Where there is a will, there is a way.

| چاهَه | chaah[a] | चाह | desire |
| راهَه | raah[a] | राह | way |

اَنڌَنِ مُلتانُ لَڌو

Andhan[i] Multaan[u] ladho

अंधनि मुल्तानु लधो

You cannot get lost on a straight road.*

اَنڌَنِ	andhan[i]	अंधनि	blind
مُلتانُ	Multaan[u]	मुल्तानु	Multan (city in Punjab)
لَڌو	ladho	लधो	found

سِجُ تِريءَ هيٺان نَہ لِڪي

Sij[u] tiree[a] hethaa[n] na like

सिजु तिरीअ हेठां न लिके

You cannot hide a light under a bushel.

سِجُ	sij[u]	सिजु	sun
هيٺان	hethaa[n]	हेठां	under
لِڪي	like	लिके	hide

ٽِنِ ۾ ٺاڪورو

Tin[i] mei[n] taakoro

टिनि में टाकोरो

Two's company, three's a crowd.

| ٺاڪورو | taakoro | टाकोरो | disturbance |

---

*The road from Hyderabad to Multan is so straight that even a blind man could undertake the journey unaided.

نَنڍِڙو ٻارُ، مُڇ جو وارُ جِيئَن وَرائيسِ تِيئَن وري

Nandh^i do baar^u, muchh jo waar^u, jeea^n waraaees^i tea^n ware

नंढिड़ो बारु, मुछ जो वारु, जीअं वराईसि, तीअं वरे

Youth and white paper take any impression.

نَنڍِڙو ٻارُ	nandh^i do baar^u	नंढिड़ो बारु	small child
مُڇَ	muchh	मुछ	moustache
وارُ	waar^u	वारु	hair
ورائيس	waraaees^i	वराईस	twist

Sindhi Proverbs That Are Culturally Unique and Have No English Equivalent

آيا مِير، ڀَڳا پِير	Aayaa meer[a], bhagaa peer	आया मीर, भगा पीर
نوڪري آهي توڪري	Nokiree aahe tokiree	नोकिरी आहे टोकिरी
نوڪر دَرَ دَرَ جا ڪُتا	Nokar[a] dar[a] dar[a] jaa kutaa	नोकर दर दर जा कुता
نوڪرُ، سونَ ۾ ٻوڙِ پِس، تَه به تُنهنجو نَه ٿِئي	Nokar[u], son[a] mein bodees[i], ta bi tu[n]hinjo na thiye	नोकरु, सोन में बोड़ीसि, त बि तुंहिंजो न थिए
مُنديءَ تي ٽِڪَ	Mundee[a] te tik[a]	मुंडी[अ] ते टिक
مِيان بيبي راضي، تو ڪيا ڪري قاضي	Miyaa[n] beebee raazee, to kyaa kare qaazee	मियां बीबी राज़ी, तो क्या करे क़ाज़ी
ڀَري ماري، ڀيرو نَه ماري	Bharee maare, bhero na maare	भरी मारे, भेरो न मारे

پيٽُ ڦاٽي، تَه اَڳِڙي
ڪيرُ وِجهي

Pet^u phaate, ta agⁱdee ker^u vijhe

पेटु फाटे, त अगिड़ी केरु विझे

هَنُ ڍَڪُ ڌِيءَ کي،
تَه سِکي نُوَنهَن

Han^u dhak^u dhee^a khe, ta sikhe noo^{nhan}

हणु धकु धीअ खे, त सिखे नूंहं

جِن جِي مَٿان
مامِرا، سي ڪِيَن
نِندُون ڪَنِ

Jinⁱ je mathaaⁿ maamⁱraa, se keeaⁿ nindooⁿ kanⁱ

जिनि जे मथां मामिरा, से कीअं निंडूं कनि

ڏِنو پيرُ، پُني مُرادَ

Ditho peer^u, punee muraad^a

डिठो पीरु, पुनी मुराद

جيڏا اُٿَ، تيڏا لوڏا

Jedaa uth^a, tedaa lodaa

जेड़ा उठ, तेड़ा लोड़ा

ماءُ گهُرِجائيتي،
ڌِيءَ واجهائيتي

Maau ghurⁱjaaitee, dhee^a vaajhaaitee

माउ घुरिजाइती, धीअ वाझाइती

سَسُ ڪاٺَ جي بِه
چَڱي، چَوي پَرَ
چَوائي نَه

Sas^u kaath^a jee bi changee, chave par^a chavaae na

ससु काठ जी बि चङी, चवे पर चवाए न

جَٽَ هُون نَه وِسَ
هُون، وِسَ هُون تَه
مُسَ هُون

Jat^a hooⁿ na vis^a hooⁿ, vis^a hooⁿ ta mus^a hooⁿ

जट हूं न विस हूं, विस हूं त मुस हूं

ماءُ ڄَڻيندي پُٽِڙا،
ڀاڳُ نَه ڏيندي وَنڌِ

Maau janeendee putⁱdaa, bhaag^u na deendee vandhⁱ

माउ जणींदी पुटिड़ा, भागु न ड्रींदी वंढि

کائبو تَه کنگهِبو

Khaaibo ta khanghⁱbo

खाइबो त खंघिबो

جَنِهنجي وَڃِجي گهَرِ، تَنِهنجي ڪَجي پَرِ (رِيتِ)	Jeⁿhinje vanyⁱje gharⁱ, teⁿhinjee kaje parⁱ (reetⁱ) जंहिंजे वञिजे घरि, तंहिंजी कजे परि (रीति)
جِنِ کاڌا پَلَنِ جا پيٽارا تِنِ جا هِينئڙا ويچارا	Jinⁱ khaadhaa palanⁱ jaa petaaraa, Tinⁱ jaa heeⁿadaa vechaaraa जिनि खाधा पलनि जा पेटारा, तिनि जा हींअड़ा वेचारा
ڪِٿي چورَ سُڄا، ڪِٿي ڍورَ سُڄا	Kithe chor^a sunyaa, kithe dhor^a sunyaaa किथे चोर सुञा, किथे ढोर सुञा
ڪو مونکي نَه وَڻي، ڪَنِهنکي آئُون نَه وَڻان	Ko muⁿkhe na vane, keⁿhiⁿkhe aauⁿ na vanaaⁿ को मुंखे न वणे, कंहिंखे आऊं न वणां
سَڀُ ڏِينهَن ڍَڪِيَلَ، عِيدَ ڏِينهُن اُگهاڙو	Sabh^u <u>d</u>eeⁿhaⁿ dhakⁱyal^a, Id^a <u>d</u>eeⁿh^{un} ughaado सभु ड़ींहं ढकियल, ईद ड़ींहुं उघाड़ो
ڀاڳُ ڏِني ڀيرو (ڏِڪو)، تَه سيري مان ٿِئي رَبَ (پَتِڙي) ڪِچِڻي	Bhaag^u <u>d</u>ie bhero (dhiko), ta seere maaⁿ thie rab^a (patⁱdee khichⁱnee) भागु ड़िए भेरो (धिको), त सीरे मां थिए रब (पतिड़ी खिचणी)
ڀاڳُ ڏِني ڀيرو (وَراڪو)، تَه دال مان ٿِئي سيرو	Bhaag^u <u>d</u>ie bhero (varaako), ta daalⁱ maan thie seero भागु ड़िए भेरो (वराको), त दालि मां थिए सीरो
ڪَسيري جي ڪُتي، ٽَڪي جا ٽُڪُرَ کائي	Kaseere jee kutee, take jaa tukur^a khaae कसीरे जी कुती, टके जा टुकुर खाए
پِني پِني مَنگل جاءُ، تَنهِن م به اَڌُ پَرائو	Pinee pinee mangal^a jaau, teⁿhⁱⁿ meiⁿ bi adh^u paraao पिनी पिनी मंगल जाउ, तंहिं में बि अधु पराओ

Athⁿ aane jee pagⁱdee, rupayo badhaanee
Kiree peyee khoohᵃ meiⁿ, ta ba rupayaa kadhaanee

अठें आने जी पगड़ी, रुपयो बधाणी
किरी पई खूह में, त ब रुपया कढाणी

Kaaneeᵃ je vihaaⁿᵃ meiⁿ sankatᵃ ghanaa

काणीअ जे विहांअ में संकट घणा

Dohitaa vadhandaa veree

डोहिटा वधंदा वेरी

Mitanⁱ chhadiyooⁿ maaitⁱyooⁿ, saganⁱ chhadiyo saahᵘ,
Ehⁱdo lago vaau, jo peⁿhinjaa bi paraavaa thiyaa

मिटनि छड़ियूं माइटियूं, सगनि छड़ियो साहु,
अहिड़ो लगो वाउ, जो पंहिंजा बि पराव थिया

Peeu sandasⁱ pehooⁿ katⁱyaa, daade sandasⁱ dhaanaa,
Age puchhandaa huaa zaatⁱ paatⁱ, haane puchhanⁱ thaa naanaa

पीउ संदसि पेहूं कटिया, डाडे संदसि धाणा,
अगे पुछंदा हुआ ज़ाति पाति, हाणे पुछनि था नाणा

Chariyanⁱ kehⁱdaa chitᵃ, muanⁱ kehⁱdaa maamⁱlaa

चरियनि कहिड़ा चित, मुअनि कहिड़ा मामिला

Jatᵃ jee jamaarᵃ, adhaee khathaa

जट जी जमार, अढाई खथा

Jeke ukh'd'yun' mein mathaa vijhan', se muh'r'yun' bhar' na dakan'

جيڪي اُکِڙِيُنِ ۾ مَٿا وِجهَنِ سي مُهرِيُنِ ڀَرِ نَه ڍَڪَنِ

जेके उखिड़ियुनि में मथा विझनि, से मुहिरियुनि भरि न ढकनि

Sen^a akhiyun' jaa nen^a

سيڻَ اَکِيُنِ جا نيڻَ

सेण अखियुनि जा नेण

Jav^a dheree, gadah^u rakh'paal^u

جَوَ ڍيري، گڏهُ رَکِپالُ

जव ढेरी, गड़हु रखिपालु

Bilee sat^a kooaa khaaee halee haj^u

ٻِلِي سَتَ ڪُوئا کائي هَلِي حَجُ

बिली सत कूआ खाई हली हजु

Bhit' te bhat^u vaahan^u

ڀِتِ تي ڀَتُ واهَڻُ

भिति ते भतु वाहणु

Jeeye muⁿhinjo shaah^u, naahe gam^u gumaash'tan' khe

جِيئي مُنهِنجو شاهُه، ناهي غَمُ گُماشِتَنِ کي

जीए मुंहिंजो शाहु, नाहे ग़मु गुमाशितनि खे

Chor^a jee maau kund^a mein roye

چورَ جي ماءُ ڪُنڊَ ۾ روئي

चोर जी माउ कुंड में रोए

Puchh'naa na munjh'naa

پُڇِڻا نَه مُنجهڻا

पुछिणा न मुंझिणा

Kar' bhalaaee jat^a saaⁿ, phere hanandui pat^a saaⁿ

ڪَرِ ڀَلائي جَٽَ سان، ڦيري هَنَنڊُءِ پَٽَ سان

करि भलाई जट सां, फेरे हणंदुइ पट सां

Par^u piyo, ghar^u viyo

پَرُ پِيو، گهَرُ وِيو

परु पियो, घरु वियो

Kad^ahiⁿ bharee^a meiⁿ, kad^ahiⁿ bhaakur^a meiⁿ

ڪَڏهِن ڀَرِيءَ ۾، ڪَڏهِن ڀاڪُرَ ۾

कड़हिं भरीअ में, कड़हिं भाकुर में

ڌوٻِيءَ جو ڪُتو، نَه گھَرَ جو نَه گھاٽَ جو	Dhobee[a] jo kuto, na ghar[a] jo na ghaat[a] jo	
	धोबी[अ] जो कुतो, न घर जो न घाट जो	
ڌوٻي ڌوئي، ڌَڻي روئي	Dhobee dhoye, dhanee roye	
	धोबी धोए, धणी रोए	
آهَ غَرِيبان قَهرُ خُدائي	Aah[a] gareebaa[n] qahir[u] khudaaee	
	आह ग़रीबां क़हिरु ख़ुदाई	
رُٺي آهي گھوٽ سان گالھائي نَٿي ڳوٺ سان	Ruthee aahe ghot[a] saa[n], gaalhaaye nathee goth[a] saa[n]	
	रुठी आहे घोट सां, ग़ाल्हाए नथी गोठ सां	
ٿَرِيو تَه دَرِياهَ، تَتو تَه تيلُ	Thar[i]yo ta dariyaah[u], tato ta tel[u]	
	ठरियो त दरियाहु, ततो त तेलु	
ڄَٹِيا پُڃَندءِ	Jan[i]yaa pujandai	
	जणिया पुजंदइ	
هِڪُ ڏي، سَو پاءِ	Hik[u] de, sau paai	
	हिकु डे, सौ पाइ	
اَبو گسي، ڌِيءَ وَسي	Abo gase, dhee[a] vase	
	अबो गसे, धी[अ] वसे	
چَمِڙي وَڃي، پَرَ دَمِڙي نَه وَڃي	Cham[i]dee vanye, par[a] dam[i]dee na vanye	
	चमिड़ी वञे, पर दमिड़ी न वञे	
ڏِنو ٻَرو ڇِنو	Dino baro chhino	
	डिनो बरो छिनो	
گَهِپي مَٽَنِ جو پاڻي سُڪائي	Gah[i]pee matan[i] jo paanee sukaaye	
	गहिपी मटनि जो पाणी सुकाए	

وَڏنِ جِي دُعا،
سُکا ڪَکَ بہ
ساوا ڪَري

Va<u>d</u>an[i] jee duaa, sukaa kakh[a] bi saavaa kare
वड़नि जी दुआ, सुका कख बि सावा करे

هِڪَ ڳِپا، تَنِھن يَر بہ لِڪانِ

Hik[a] gipaa, te[n]hi[n] bhar[i] bi likaa[n]
हिक गिपा, तंहिं भरि बि लिकां

بُرقعي ۾ سُرڪو

Burqe mei[n] surko
बुर्क़े में सुर्क़ो

رَنگَ ۾ ڀَنگُ

Rang[a] mei[n] bhang[u]
रंग में भंगु

اَڻَ گھَڙِيو ڪاٽُ

An[a] gha<u>d</u>[i]yo kaath[u]
अण घड़ियो काठु

دالِ، بَچِڙا پالِ

Daal[i], <u>b</u>achidaa paal[i]
दालि, बचिड़ा पालि

پَنھنجي ڳَتيءَ پَوَ گڏَھَ کي پيري

Pe[n]hinjee gatee[a] pau ga<u>d</u>ah[a] khe pere
पंहिंजी गतीअ पउ गड़ह खे पेरे

ڏِنو پُٽُ ڇُٽي جو

<u>D</u>ino put[u] chhute jo
ड़िनो पुटु छुटे जो

جيتِرا ماڻھُو، اوتِريوُن ڳالھِيوُن

Jet[i]raa maanhoo, ot[i]r[i]yoo[n] gaalh[i]yoo[n]
जेतिरा माण्हू, ओतिरियूं गा़ल्हियूं

مُڙَسُ تَہ قَڏو، نَہ تَہ جَڏو

Mud[u]s[u] ta pha<u>d</u>o, na ta ja<u>d</u>o
मुड़सु त फड़ो, न त जड़ो

اَڪيلانِيءَ کي بَنِيھہ (32) جِنَ

Akelaaee[a] khe <u>b</u>ateeh[a] jin[a]
अकेलाई^अ खे बटीह जिन

اُٿَ مَٿان وِڃِڻي

Uth[a] mathaa[n] vinyinee
उठ मथां विजिणी

196 • Sindh Bani

اُٿُ پُنۡيان گھنڊِنيٖن	Uth^a puth^{i}yaan^n ghind^{i}nee^n	
	उठ पुठियां घिंडिणी	
پُٽُ پينگھي مٖ پڌِرو	Put^u peenghe mein padh^{i}ro	
	पुटु पींघे में पधिरो	
وَقتَ ڪَيو واڪو،	Vaqt^a kayo vaako, ta ghode ga<u>d</u>aha khe kayo kaako	
تَه گھوڙي گَڏَهَ		
کي ڪَيو ڪاڪو		
	वक़्त कयो वाको, त घोड़े ग<u>ड</u>ह खे कयो काको	
ماسي ٿِئي نَه ماءُ،	Maasee thie na maa^u, tode kadhee <u>d</u>ie saah^u	
توڙي ڪَڍي ڏِني ساهُه		
	मासी थिए न माउ, तोड़े कढी <u>ड</u>िए साहु	
عامِلُ، کُٽَلُ بِه خانُ	Aamil^u, khutal^u bi khaan^u	
	आमिलु, खुटलु बि ख़ानु	
ڌِيئَڙي سو ڪَرِ	Dheeadee so kar^i, jo <u>d</u>ithui maau ghar^i	
جو ڏِٺُئه ماءُ گھَرِ	Noo^{n}ha^{n}dee so kar^i, jo <u>d</u>ithui sas^u ghar^i	
نُونھَڙي سو ڪَرِ		
جو ڏِٺُئه سَسُ گھَرِ		
	धीअड़ी सो करि, जो <u>ड</u>िठुइ माउ घरि,	
	नूंहड़ी सो करि, जो <u>ड</u>िठुइ ससु घरि	
ناٺي، ڏِنگي ڪاٺي	Naathee, <u>d</u>ingee kaathee	
	नाठी, <u>ड</u>िंगी काठी	
ناني رَڌَنَ واري،	Naanee radhan^a vaaree, <u>d</u>ohitaa khaain^a vaaraa	
ڏوھِتا کائڻ وارا		
	नानी रधण वारी, <u>ड</u>ोहिता खाइण वारा	
سينَنِ جو ڏِنو،	Senan^i jo <u>d</u>ino, saanvan^a jo meenh^{un}	
سانوَنَ جو مِينهُن		
	सेणनि जो <u>ड</u>िनो, सांवण जो मींहु	
ڏِني مَٿان،	<u>D</u>ie mathaa^n, ke^{n}hinje hathaa^n	
ڪنھنجي ھَٿان		
	<u>ड</u>िए मथां कंहिंजे हथां	

لِپي عَقُلُ نَہ چِي پُنَهلَ، آئوُنْ بہ کِنِ سَنگِ گڏِیَسِ

Labhe aqulu na, che 'Punhala, aaun bi kini sangi gadiyasi'

लभे अकुलु न, चे 'पुन्हल, आउं बि किनि संगि गडियसि'

عَقُلُ	aqulu	अकुलु	wisdom
پُنَهل	Punhala	पुन्हल	Punhal (Name of a person)
گڏِیَسِ	gadiyasi	गडियसि	in the company of

198 • Sindh Bani

SIND
BEAUTIFUL - SWEET & LOVABLE MOTHERLAND OF SINDHIS

Sindhwork and Sindhworkis

Tekchand Karamchand Mirchandani

Translation
Sarla Nari Kripalani

Foreword

There is an urgent need at this time for the book *Sindhwork and Sindhworkis*. What is Sindhwork? And who is a Sindhworki? There were some people who wanted to be knowledgeable about Sindhwork so they would pick a story from here or a statement from there, and form an opinion. Even the Sindhworkis, who spent their whole life in business, were themselves not sure of their foundation.

The author of this book has made every effort to portray an honest image of the Sindhworki Sethias. He has not meant to hurt or falsify, but in his enthusiasm he has related instances that many of my brethren may not approve of. One can say the writer has mentioned many shortcomings of the Sethias that may or may not apply to the community as a whole. The writer hopes that the Sindhworki Sethias and the Bhaiband community will rise to the occasion and work towards the betterment of the community.

The system is woven in bright colours, but the etchings are cut deep—change will not be easy. What the writer can hope for is that the Sindhworki and Bhaiband youth, who will one day head their forefathers' business houses, may open their minds and change the system; and be more patriotic to the community and the province from which they hail.

The book has not brought out the best in the Sindhworkis nor has it provided any solutions. I pray to God that the hopes of the writer be fulfilled and the idea with which he has set out to write this book is not misunderstood. So do not look upon him in anger. Instead, consider this book to be his way of showing love for his country and the Sindhi community.

—Shyamdas Naraindas Chulani
1 November 1919

Author's Note

Ten years ago I decided to write about the lives of Sindhworkis and present it to the general public. No sooner was the decision made than I put pen to paper. I was a little afraid to be critical of such a powerful and courageous community. I did not think myself capable of doing so. I wrote the first draft but did not think much of it. I wrote a second draft but eventually discarded it and decided to give up the idea.

Day by day, as I witnessed the gradual decline in the mentality of the Sindhworki community, I decided to take up the task once more. This time I was successful. I realized that I was an amateur writer but took courage and made a humble attempt in the hope that a more capable person will better it. I know of no Sindhworki who is educated or experienced enough to guide me. It is quite likely that I have been mistaken in many instances.

I request the community's leaders to overlook my simple Sindhi and to sift the grain from the chaff, and to grasp the essence and intent with which this book has been written. Not being a man of letters I am unable to resort to flowery language and phrasing. At times I have had to resort to harsh words about the Sindhworki community because I feel they are in such deep sleep that unless they themselves feel the pinch, it will be impossible to wake them from their slumber. After reading this book, I hope the Sindhworki powers-that-be will be a little bit tender towards their people and rejoice in the betterment of their prospects.

I request my Sindhworki Sethia brethren that when they read this book, if there are any shortcomings, to please present them clearly to the common man so that whatever untoward gossip they might have heard about the Sindhworki Sethias is wiped out from their hearts and minds.

The request is for the man on the street and not their servants, employees and partners. Before I sent this book out into the world, I showed it to a friend of mine, Bhai Shyamdas Naraindas, who has given his own opinion, and which I have presented to the readers as the Foreword.

—**Tekchand Karamchand Mirchandani**
Hyderabad, Sindh

How Did the Word 'Sindhworki' Originate?

In the year 1843, when the British took over the rule of Sindh, Hyderabad became its capital city, and artisans from across the region flocked there in search of a livelihood. Budding entrepreneurs would take artefacts from door to door and sell them to English households.

The first question the foreigners asked was, 'Is this made in Sindh?' The reply would always be in the affirmative. When the young salesmen realized that anything made in Sindh was desirable to the English, they began to lead with the question, 'Do you want to see Sindh work?' Hence the door-to-door salesmen came to be known as Sindhworkis, i.e. those selling articles made in Sindh. Over time, the name became synonymous with any businessman from Sindh.

Though they have now gone farther and spread all over the world, they are still known as Sindhworkis—those who left the shores of their motherland with articles made in Sindh and made their fortunes abroad.

02 The Spread of Sindhworkis

Sindhworki salesmen earned quite a lot from the foreigners, and more and more people entered the trade. Some got the bright idea of going out of Sindh to sell their wares. The first stop was Bombay, which was the British stronghold. The first immigrants to Bombay called themselves 'Sethias' and employed younger men to roam the city and sell their products. The Sethias found out that a large English population had also congregated in Egypt and the Strait Settlements. So the Sethia Bhai Pohumal set sail for Egypt and Bhai Vasiamal for the Straits Settlements. When they touched ground and found a firm footing, they sent for their salesmen in Bombay and set up offices in these new lands. Others learnt of the pots of gold at the end of the rainbow and trade prospered, soon spreading all over the world. Many new Sethias entered the fray.

03 The Advantage of Sindhwork

It would not be out of place to mention that a substantial section of Hyderabad was earning its livelihood from Sindhwork and thousands of families were dependent on it. Besides which, thousands more were employed by the Sethias and at least Rs 2,00,000 was paid out in salaries each month. Apart from this, the Sethias and their partners earned an additional Rs 5,00,000 to Rs 6,00,000 as their share of the profits. These were cash profits shared by the Hyderabad Sethias, but the real big money was outside Sindh and in the cities of India.

Many different handicrafts from all over India were sent to be sold outside India only through the Sindhworkis. Many crafts were kept alive only because of the Sindhworkis, otherwise it would not have been possible for these to be exported. (The Sethias, or Bhais, reaped huge profits and expanded into big business houses.) Thanks to these handicrafts, thousands of craftsmen made their living. Hence, not just us Sindhis, but many craftsmen all over India are indebted to the Sindhworkis, who undertook great personal risks and travelled abroad to make money and bring it back to invest in their own country.

04 The Moving Salesman

The foundation of Sindhwork was based on moving salesmen and to this day they play an important role in the setting up of a business.

When a Sindhworki starts business in a new city or country, his first step is *pherie*, i.e. a roaming salesmanship with minimal investment. The advantages of starting as a pherie are:

(1) The salesman is master and servant rolled into one, so there is no expenditure involved. He does not have to invest in premises or engage any staff; the few articles on his back and the profits are all his own.
(2) He can be cautious, feel the pulse of the city and find out whether his goods have a market value or not.
(3) Since he may not be familiar with the language, ways and customs of the people, by merely meeting a lot of people he picks up the language quickly and can assess the likes and dislikes of the people.
(4) By roaming from quarter to quarter and marketplace to shopping centre, the salesman comes to know which is the best place to set up shop and where it will be most profitable.

In short, no business was possible for a Sindhworki unless he started out as a pherie. To this day the rule holds good and therefore a crisis can be averted.

05 Advantages of Pherie

No Sindhworki worth his name can say he started out as a Sethia. He was first a *pheriewallah* and then engaged a servant who did the hard work. Only then could he call himself a 'Sethia'.

When the Sethias started setting up offices outside India, they needed hard-working staff. However, people were reluctant to go. The Sethias would often employ simple men from the less privileged class and treat them virtually like slaves. The treatment meted out to them would send shivers down the spine of listeners. The slave of a salesman was duty-bound to serve his master, the Sethia, for 24 hours in a day, if so required. No thought was given to his food, clothing, living quarters, and rest was unheard of.

Early in the morning, the salesman would take a heavy bundle on his shoulders and make the rounds of the city. He would reach home in the evening, cook his meals, eat, clean up and set out again to sell his wares; returning only at midnight or even later, in the wee hours of the morning.

On the occasion of the arrival of a new consignment, he would be required to open, sort and make bundles of the goods. It would take the best part of the night and by the time he was done it would be time once again to be off on his pherie. This relentless routine could continue for three, four or even five years before he would earn enough for a return fare to visit his family.

If an employee made a mistake he would be beaten black and blue. It was an unwritten law that a Sethia could treat his employees as he wished to and no one dared intervene. The monthly salary would typically be between Rs 10 and Rs 20, along with a miscellaneous allowance of Rs 20 to Rs 25. The Sethia would keep the rest of the profit, which amounted to about Rs 1,000 per month.

The Sethias, who were lucky to get such beasts of burden for a pittance, became rich overnight.

06 Taking Advantage of Sindhworki Partners

I don't think anywhere in the world could Sethias get partners at as low a percentage of profits as they did here in Sindh. This does not mean that those partners who drove a hard bargain were a bad deal for the Sethias—not at all! The Sethias were so smart that they would twist and turn the words of the contract and ultimately get the grain, while the partners got the chaff. Even then, the partners were at the mercy of the Sethias for the stipulated period.

Such Sethias lived in the lap of luxury. When, what and how they paid their partners was not questioned by the head of the community or relatives or friends, as the contract was between the Sethia and the partner who paid the initial money. But it was the partner who was left holding the beggar's bowl.

The Advantage of Sindhworki Illiteracy

In every walk of life there are advantages and disadvantages. It is left to the reader to discern these, keeping in view the lifestyle, customs and other practices of the country. Everyone is welcome to their own opinion.

Bhaiband means brother-in-trade. Had they been literate they would not have done pherie or worked as roving salesmen, which was considered lowly work in those days. The foundation of Sindhwork is pherie, hence the Bhaiband class remained illiterate. However, their business acumen was remarkable. They were the brains behind the business houses and more savvy in many ways than men of letters.

There were many Bhaibands who aspired for their children to be well educated. But after achieving this goal, they were sorely disappointed as the children, instead of joining their forefathers' business, refused to live within the joint family. Instead, they left the fold for the 'Amil' community, which was highly educated, and hence very respected. The Amils were the professional class, Indian civil servants and government officers, who often looked down on traders with contempt.

In Hyderabad, one can see people clothed in an array of caps, turbans and dhotis, which is an integral part of the Bhaiband community's traditional appearance. Their less-educated children continue to acknowledge the elders as the heads of their family, give them due respect and help them in their trade.

Reasons Why Sindhworki Children Were Illiterate

(1) Bhaiband children do not consider it degrading to be uneducated, as around them they see their parents and relatives who did not go to school. Hence the desire to study takes a back seat.
(2) Parents—more so fathers—are unable to supervise their children's education since they are away from home for long periods. The mothers, being illiterate, are unable to help.
(3) The young ones, seeing their neighbours wearing gold rings, chains and fancy watches, started to perform poorly in school because they wanted to become Sindhworkis and make money to gain material comforts.
(4) Likewise, parents associated with Bhaibands saw that youngsters could make a lot of money with Sindhwork, away from home, so they did not pressurize their children to study. By the time they reached fourth standard and entered adolescence, many dropped out of school, and there were only a handful that passed their matriculation examination that would have allowed them to pursue higher education. Only one or two Bhaiband children reached that stage.

09 Reasons for Illiteracy of Sethia Children

As children, the Sethia's family had heard that it was useless to study because ultimately you would be joining your father's business so why wrack your brains and waste money on education. Money will follow you wherever you set up offices with your father. Education is necessary only up to the point that you learn to read and write and converse in English so as to attend to customers, prepare bills and write cheques. Moreover if you have a well-versed clerk, then you need not even do that. Sindhwork families would often encourage their friends to send their sons to work for them to earn money, travel and become 'smart'—which they did! These boys blended in with the local people, picked up their languages and even married their girls.

10 For Correspondence and Bookkeeping, the Clerical Staff Must Be Bhaiband and Not Amil

After some time, as their business expanded, the Sindhworkis found it increasingly difficult to manage their accounts.

The Bhaibands were so afraid of the Amils that they would look for a Bhaiband clerk. An Amil looked down his nose at an illiterate man and had little regard for the way the Sethia treated his subordinates and considered it 'moral suffering.' Because of this the Bhaiband would often take a dig at the Amil and if he employed one, would take great pleasure in ordering him to do work that was below his status or even ask him to do something illegal, which the Amil would not put up with and he would immediately reply in the negative. The poor manager would then be at a loss. This was not the offspring of a Bhaiband—who can be bullied into doing whatever was required of them. The Amil was well-versed in legal matters and knew his rights and could fight for them. The Bhaiband boy, however, would be really frightened that the Sethia who had sponsored him and taken his signature on documents could drag him to court and put a noose around his neck. So he would quietly send for money from home and go back to his family. Even in his own country he would not speak against the atrocities and injustices of the Sethia nor dare to sue the Sethia heirs.

The Jealousies among Sindhworkis

All Sindhworkis have an inherent streak of jealousy. No matter how much they admire their colleagues, at the end of it all, they would add a 'but'—'...but he is a very jealous man'. Meaning the person being spoken about cannot bear to see another person do well, especially if that person does better than himself.

For instance, if there is a factory, industry, business already in existence and the proprietor, Mr A, has done very well, the next person, Mr B, will not be able to tolerate his reaching the zenith. Mr B will go all out to see that Mr A comes to nought. Mr B will call his most cunning and experienced pheriewallahs to shadow Mr A's pheriewallahs and undersell similar goods, even at a loss to himself. If such tactics don't work, he will provoke a quarrel, leading to partners of both the rival firms landing up at the police station. So for the time being, Mr A is at a loss even though Mr B is sustaining greater losses.

There are innumerable ways of destroying the competition. If the above fails, Mr B could strike up a false friendship with Mr A—invite him home to dinner and get him so drunk that Mr A will reveal confidential business information. Mr B will then instruct his men to intercept the next consignment. When the steamer docks, they will first try to bribe the chief officer. If the chief officer is an honest Joe, they will bribe the sailors and steal all of Mr A's goods.

If someone comes to know that a certain firm is putting a shop up for rent, or that a lease has expired and Mr X is negotiating for it, Mr Y will offer a higher rent just to block Mr X's deal. This way Mr Y will be at a loss, Mr X is denied the deal and a third party takes away the profits; but Mr Y's Sindhworki satisfaction lies in the fact that Mr X's Sindhwork has gone down the drain.

If Firm A sends a consignment of goods to a new agent—for which Firm B has been secretly trying to deal with for the last three months—and Firm B comes to know of Firm A's dealings, Firm B will not rest until Firm A's consignment deal is destroyed. A story goes that in the holy town of Kashi, those who were unsuccessful in life would commit suicide in the precincts of a particular temple, believing their spirit would rise to Heaven. In the same vein, Firm B will not hesitate to undergo heavy monetary losses and face all trials and tribulations. It may even knowingly risk having its own staff embezzle lakhs of rupees in the process, since it is only their word on the amount spent over the tussle. But the joy of the Sethia of Firm B will know no bounds that Firm A has at last been ruined, and the Sethia of Firm B will not even struggle with his own conscience or have any regret—not an iota!

If a customer goes to a shop with a parcel and the salesman recognizes the package as belonging to a competitor's shop, he will, come hell or high water, manage to steal a look at the goods. After doing so he will send a junior salesman to procure identical goods, find out the price and undersell the items by Rs 5 to Rs 8 and wean away the customers, even at a loss to himself! But the delight he experiences more than makes up for the loss!!

Some Sindhworkis of days gone by would say that this jealousy and this behaviour kept alive the Sindhwork as without this keen competition and ups and downs of trade the Sethias and firms would have stagnated.

 Alcoholism among Sindhworkis

In the previous chapter we came to know how Sindhworki Sethias and the partners of rival firms engaged in a cold war with each other. Their main pleasure was bringing about the destruction of their competitors. This gave a chance to the pheriewallahs and other staff members to escape from the slavery of the Sethias. As new companies mushroomed, the senior staff got more importance. The lack of proper boarding and lodging forced the pheriewallahs to eat out.

The Sethias and their managers pretended to take no notice of it. The former fixed a price for the goods that the pheriewallahs sold for the firm. By and by the pheriewallahs learnt the tricks of the trade and sold the goods at a higher price than that fixed by the managers, and pocketed the difference themselves. They began to indulge in various pleasures, starting with alcohol, and felt that over a round of drinks, tongues loosened and profits were made.

The Sethias again turned a Nelson's eye, a deaf ear and remained tight-lipped, because so many companies now sprang up that were willing to take on experienced labour—the pheriewallahs. The former slaves of the firm knew he could easily and immediately get another job and would be daring enough to hand in his resignation. Times had changed and alcohol was considered a necessary evil both to make friends and destroy foes.

13. The Outcome of Alcoholism

Alcohol is not a product that can be confined within boundaries. As it became available to the staff, their desire to consume it increased even more. Though the managers fixed a certain quota for the staff, force of habit made them consume more. They would keep a limited amount at home but have a few drinks outside. The managers ignored it at first but then began deducting the full cost of alcohol from the pheriewallahs' earnings. How long could an alcoholic continue to work and earn? They brought in less and less income until, ultimately, the Sethias stopped employing pheriewallahs.

Thus the pheriewallah system died a natural death. If at all one sees them in today's times, they are not employed by the Sethias but are self-employed, having started their businesses on a small scale.

14 Wealth at All Costs

Sindhworkis are very fond of making money. Human nature desires wealth but the Sindhworki motto is 'wealth at all costs'—no matter if he has to trample on others while doing so. The glitter of gold makes him forget his manners and his moral duties towards mankind. He will not consider his partners, managers, employees at any level who helped him make the millions which he enjoys. The staff can go and die in a ditch as far as he is concerned. The community, which was born in jealousy and lived in jealousy, cannot be expected to have a conscience.

Many were the youngsters who worked hard for the Sethias in the hope of a better life. But the Sethia squeezed out their livelihood and exploited them during their youth, only to dump them like gutter rats in their old age, with not a penny for them or their families.

15 Reasons for the Lack of Savings

In this chapter we shall attempt to expose and justify the allegations against the Sethias. In the good old days, the Sethias used to tell their pheriewallahs that on no account must the latter sell certain items at prices lower than what was fixed by the former. Salesmen who sold the goods over and above the price fixed by the Sethias were patted on the back and told that they 'were hard-working and would go far'; and that they were 'well thought of' if not actually respected. Thus it became an unwritten custom for the pheriewallah to give the Sethias more than the fixed price. The Sethia would say, 'your good work will not be wasted and the final reckoning will be at the end of the journey,' i.e. the end of the contract.

The salesman's pay for the very first contract or 'journey', as it was termed—which could last anywhere between two and four years—was rarely more than Rs 25 per month. Of this, Rs 15 would be sent to his family, and the young man would keep the remaining Rs 10 for himself. No matter how frugally he spent that money, it was impossible to save more than Rs 100 to Rs 150 at the end of his journey.

At the end of a three-year contract, if ill health had not depleted his bank balance, the savings of Rs 150 would be spent on buying gifts for his family and friends back home. Sindhworkis were expected to return from abroad loaded with money. So to put on a false show, the salesman would borrow money from the Sethia for his holiday, banking on the promises of *lungi-poti* at the end of the contract.

The Sethias were a sly lot and would ask the pheriewallah to sign a second contract, failing which the latter must pay off the debt, as the bonuses were insufficient to cover his expenses. Out of desperation he would sign up for another journey and so the cycle would continue. The salesman was thus pushed into living another three years in slavery.

16 The True Story of a Salesman: An Autobiography

My first contract: I was put behind the counter at a Sethia's shop. It was not the long hours that bothered me but the treatment meted out. If, by chance, I made a mistake, or if a customer asked for something I was not able to locate immediately, or if the customer left the shop without purchasing anything, the heavens would fall upon me. The Sethia would pick up anything he could lay his hands on and throw it at me. I would bleed and even fainted many times from the physical assault. Yet no one dared come to my rescue.

Abuse was like a shower of rose petals in comparison. My colleagues and I worked at the shop until midnight or 1 a.m., and often even until 2 or 3 in the morning. After that, we used to spread our bedding on the damp shop floor and try to sleep. This was easier said than done, as we were also the night watchmen and had the responsibility of grappling with any thieves, should they break into the shop. In any case, the dampness did not allow us to sleep, and fevers and coughs were common. Medical expenses were added to our accounts, with the result that our meagre pay seldom allowed for any savings.

At the time, the pheriewallah's life seemed wonderful. At least they had the liberty of being outdoors in the sunlight and fresh air. One day, having pleased my Sethia, I requested—with a thudding heart and folded hands—that I be allowed to take on the pheriewallah's job. The Sethia was in a good mood and agreed. My happiness knew no bounds.

Every day I would go out, sell my wares and return with more money than required by the contract. I handed it all over to the Sethia and felt proud of a job well done. Every week, the manager checked our accounts. My sales consistently exceeded expectations and I felt happy that all the profits were being safely kept for me until I went back home.

Somewhere along the line, some goods went missing, but the Sethia just gave me a warning and asked me to be more careful the next time I opened my bundles. Any such losses were deducted from my account.

I struck up a friendship with another salesman on the same beat. He was an old hand and advised me that I shouldn't hand over all extra earnings to the Sethia. He said that if goods are stolen again or the accounts are not clear, the losses will be deducted from my share and at the end of the journey I will have nothing left. 'What will you take home? A debt?' he warned. 'The Sethia will not keep the extras for you but for himself, and will see to it that you are indebted to him and force you to sign another contract. If you want to change jobs, you will not be able to do so because the Sethia will tell you that you have already spent all your extras on medical bills, stolen goods, etc. Do not be naïve, and save the extras for yourself and your family.'

That night I could not sleep. Where could I keep the extra money? If I carried it on my person and the Sethia decided to search my pockets, I would be in a soup. If I kept it in my suitcase and he searched the suitcase, he would brand me a thief. Not only would he take away my job but he would inform all the other firms not to engage me and I would have to return home dishonoured.

In disgust, I threw away the day's extra earnings into a drain.

On my way to the shop I felt very sad that my hard-earned money had been wasted.

The next day I made it a point to meet another experienced pheriewallah, an older man who I felt would guide me. He asked me to return a little earlier from my rounds and meet him at a certain coffee shop.

When I entered, I was astounded to see not only the person who had asked me to come but also pheriewallahs from my firm, my own colleagues. It was a party! They welcomed me and were very cordial. Would you believe it, readers, that ever since my contract, this was the first time I had good food and my fill of it!

When it was time to go, everyone took out the day's earnings, keeping only the contractual amount to give to the Sethias. They advised me to take out more than the contract money, as all these months I had been giving the Sethia practically double of what I was supposed to give him. The salesmen told me to gradually give less and less until I reached the contract limit. This way the Sethia would not suspect anything. All extra earnings were collected by the proprietor of the coffee shop until it was time for us to return home.

The salesmen then left the coffee shop, one by one, so that nobody would suspect anything. If the Sethia should see two pheriewallahs going about together or being friendly, he would beat the daylights out of them.

Life became easier and I had a place to rest and chit-chat with fellow human beings. One day, one of the pheriewallahs got a bright idea. He said, 'Tomorrow is Sunday. Let us take "French leave" and enjoy ourselves. From today's earnings, we will give only half (or whatever was fixed for the day) to the Sethia, and tomorrow we take our bundles as usual, but instead of working, we meet at the coffee shop and at the end of the day give the other half of today's earnings. The Sethia will be none the wiser.' The motion was unanimously applauded and, with bonhomie, we started spending every Sunday at the coffee shop. The proprietor was also happy that so many people would be eating at his shop and his earnings also augmented.

Time went on and my contract came to an end. I was ready to return home. The manager of the firm put a proposal before me—if I stayed on for another 12 months, my pay would go up from Rs 25 per month to Rs 40 per month.

I decided to take the offer.

At the coffee shop it was decided that instead of only Sunday, we would also have another mid-week holiday on Thursdays. But two rest days became too much and for want of something to do, we started playing cards and soon with stakes to keep the monotony at bay.

The stipulated twelve months came to an end and I returned home. I calculated that the Rs 15 increment had sufficed for my indulgences. I bought from Bombay a four-poster bed, a fancy mirror and gifts for everyone in Hyderabad. The manager gave me the advance without cribbing and the Sethia agreed to a further advance of Rs 200, which was sufficient to live in Sindhworki style for at least two months.

During this period, I repeatedly asked the Sethia to clear my account. Each time the reply would be, 'The manager has not yet sent the accounts, but if you require any money, feel free to ask.'

I had a nagging feeling that there was more to it than met the eye and until I saw the accounts, I would take no more money. Ultimately, after a couple of months, when the Sethia felt I was well rested and might be looking for another job contract, he asked me when I would like to sign the agreement for the next journey. I told him to show me the accounts, the credits and debits and the bonuses promised, and then I would decide.

The Sethia said, 'All that will be done by and by, but you think of signing the next contract.' I agreed and the next day, an agreement of terms and conditions was typed out on stamp paper. I demanded a pay of Rs 80 per month based on my four years of experience. Bhai wanted me to accept Rs 40. I refused. Bhai bargained for Rs 60 per month. I was adamant and, calling his bluff, told him that so and so firm is offering me Rs 80. Bhai was very angry and abused me and said, 'I shall see which firm takes you on!' He ordered his accountant to prepare my balance sheet. To my horror, I found that I had an outstanding debt of almost Rs 500 in addition to Rs 200 for lost articles during my pherie. My pay for the whole journey had been calculated at Rs 25 per month!

I went to the accountant and told him I was promised an increment of Rs 15 and the loss was only Rs 50 or Rs 60, which the manager had assured me he would not deduct since I brought in more money than contracted for the daily pherie.

The Sethia brought out the agreement and asked me to show him the proof of Rs 40 that was promised. Of course, there was none. I had trusted them and learned my lesson that everything must be put in writing.

The Sethia threatened to file a suit against me if I did not return the money within the next two or three days.

I returned home and related the happenings of the day to my parents. They were flabbergasted. Where would I get the princely sum of Rs 700–800? And over and above that, lawyer's fees and the ignominy—no firm would trust a person who had gone to court!

My father immediately went to see the Sethia, and with folded hands begged him not to file a suit. The Sethia told him he would wipe out all outstanding debts if I would accept Rs 60 per month and sign the agreement for a further three years. I was trapped into another journey.

I was fortunate that the manager gave me a job at the shop. Times had changed and now a job behind the counter was considered more prestigious than the pherie.

I was surprised to see the demeanour and manners of the pheriewallahs. They had taken to alcohol, drinking at every meal. No sooner did the Sethia leave the house, the pheriewallahs would hold a *darbar* and festivities took place in the house. Previously we met secretly at the coffee shop. Now they frequented the coffee shop to gamble—every day!

One day's gambling at the coffee shop sometimes left the boys with nothing to give to the Sethias at the end of the day and they would hang their heads in shame. Now they were bold enough to come before the manager dead drunk and without any earnings for three to four days.

If the manager asked them why they had not come in every day, they would answer, 'If there is no business, do you want us to steal and bring you money?' Again, if they were questioned as to where they got the money for drinks, pat came the reply, 'Tell the Sethia to look after his pheries and see that the contract is in order, or else…' Obviously the Sethias were not at a loss in spite of all this, so the pheriewallahs stayed.

The new pherie recruits did not have much experience and soon fell prey to the ways of the experienced ones. After doing some business, they would go to the coffee shop and gamble. It came to pass that when they lacked funds, they started gambling with the bolts of silk and other items in their custody which, regretfully, belonged to the Sethias. The reader can well evaluate the losses the Bhai suffered. Some people found the courage to tell the Sethia to do away with the pheriewallahs, given the losses. The Sethia replied, 'If the other firms do it, so will I.' It was considered prestigious to have pheriewallahs—the larger the number, the more important the firm!

As time went by, and as contracts came to an end, all the firms did away with their pheriewallahs and took to wholesale export businesses or set up beautiful local shops, which the Sethias could manage with a small, reliable staff.

17 Sethias Deliberately Ruined the Pheriewallah System

Dear reader, you may find it difficult to believe that the Sethias, who earned lakhs of rupees from the pheriewallahs, ended up strangling the system with their own hands. But reality cannot be denied, and the truth inevitably comes to light.

I was present at a Sindhworki meeting where an argument broke out between two persons. I remember what was said verbatim, and will relate it to you. It is not advisable to reveal the real names, lest their Sethias direct their wrath at them, so I will use substitutes.

> **Panjumal:** Day by day, Sindhworkis are taking more and more to hard liquor. I wonder what is the reason.
> **Bherumal:** The reason? We follow in the footsteps of our leaders. They must have thought something good would come of drinking.
> **Panjumal:** These so-called leaders are neither your ancestors nor heads of your panchayat.
> **Bherumal:** Who cares for those old fogies in Hyderabad, living like frogs in a well that do not know anything about the outside world? I am talking of the Sethias, who went around

the world and earned so much money.

Panjumal: Have they found some virtue in alcohol in the West?

Bherumal: Virtue or vice, I cannot say, but we are their paid servants and since we spend the whole day with them so we have to do as they desire.

Panjumal: When you were in Hyderabad, you never used to drink?

Bherumal: I used to detest alcohol, but since I've started Sindhwork, it has become a habit. There, liquor was a daily affair and I could not refuse it in a large gathering. Then I thought, 'I am getting this for free. Why not find out if it is pleasurable?' Now it is a habit.

Panjumal: I am surprised. What did people achieve by giving hard liquor to the Sindhworkis?

Bherumal: Initially, it was a gesture of goodwill. If the Sethia poured out a peg for his subordinate, the person so singled out would pay more attention to the business in hand to make more profits. For those who were habituated, it saved them from spending their own money on a drink at a bar.

Panjumal: You mean to say all Sindhworkis who leave Hyderabad are drunkards?

Bherumal: No. As a matter of fact, those who left Hyderabad for the first time did not even know the taste of liquor. But getting free drinks and seeing others enjoy themselves, one soon acquires a taste for it.

Panjumal: How much does a Sethia spend for each staff member's liquor?

Bherumal: It depends on the country. In some places liquor is very expensive and in others, it costs a pittance.

Panjumal: As a guess—could it be Rs 5–7 per month?

Bherumal: That must be so, per servant.

Panjumal: What do you mean 'per servant'? [In those days, they were indeed referred to as 'servants' and treated as menials.] What about the partners and managers? Do their expenses exceed that?

Bherumal: There is no limit for partners and managers. Their expense on liquor is not listed, so one cannot say. Some partners are teetotallers while others consume a bottle within two days, or maybe at one sitting. Some managers' pay is Rs 60 per month yet their liquor bill is Rs 70 per month.

Panjumal: Are your Sethias aware of all this?

Bherumal: Sethias have no time to check on these petty expenses. Suffice to say that a certain manager is a drunkard and the other drinks within reason. The managers show their liquor bills as 'within reason' and the extra, they enter under 'other items' to balance accounts.

Panjumal: Anyway, now that these 'servants' drink at home, they could not be going out for drinks?

Bherumal: At first they were confined to their homes. But now they go out. The Sethias know that their pheriewallahs are wasting money, but they stay silent.

Panjumal: The Sethias suffer losses and still neither advise them nor pull them up?

Bherumal: Now they are beyond control. Moreover, the Sethia who himself drinks like a fish is hardly considered a good enough person to advise others.

Panjumal: Why don't the Sethias sack such drunkards? It's a bad example for new recruits.

Bherumal: The Sethias lack foresight. If the servant or Sindhworki earns for him, well and good. His personal life is irrelevant. The moment business suffers—that is, if the profits drop—the servant will get the royal boot! There are enough servants who earn Rs 1,000, spend Rs 500 on vices and hand over the balance Rs 500 to the Sethia with all humility and thereby earn the goodwill of the Sethia along with bonuses, promotions, increments as well as free liquor.

Panjumal: If such is the situation that a large portion of funds disappear under the Sethia's nose, and he still parts with bonuses and gives promotions to the staff, there must be quite a few rascals who live by dishonest means?

Bherumal: That way, the Sindhwork Sethias are like hawks. When their worker reaches Hyderabad, they have their belongings searched and God forbid if the presents, etc., brought by the member exceeds their pay (which means they have pilfered funds), he will be made an outcaste and no one will employ him again—no matter how good a salesman he is or how much more he can earn for the Sethia. Even if it is beyond the contracted amount.

Panjumal: This means the Sindhworki Sethias encourage their staff to drink even at the cost of monetary loss to themselves and be a blot on their reputation? I fail to understand what they gain? If they discipline their staff, they would stand to profit!

Bherumal: The servants were simple people. Had the Sethias given them commission on sales or 50 per cent of the monies earned over and above the contract, the employees would have accounted for each and every paaee. The Sethias would profit and the employee would remain virtuous and loyal.

Panjumal: Why did the Sethias not think of this kind of a deal?

Bherumal: If you think it did not occur to the Sethias, you are sadly mistaken. They have travelled all over the world and gained experience. They thought this would be a raw deal and they will lose much more.

Panjumal: I gather that pheries and pheriewallahs are outdated? By and large it is a closed system and very soon will become extinct? Could you enumerate how and why this system of business should die, when the Sethias were making lakhs of rupees from it?

Bherumal: Listen, if the Sethias had given their pheriewallahs a commission of 50 per cent of the profits, at the end of each journey, i.e. a contract of three years, their pheriewallahs would have been entitled to a minimum of Rs 2,000–2,500. When the Sethias took them on for work at Rs 25 per month and the pheriewallahs were virtually their slaves, why would they allow them the taste of independence?

The pheriewallahs were called servants because they were not only roving salesmen, but also watchmen, cooks, gofers, masseurs, all rolled into one. The Sethia just had to snap his fingers and the most menial job was done—all for the price of practically nothing. The other way, if the pheriewallah got Rs 2,000–4,000 in hand, would he not be able to open his own shop and do business with the experience of that one contracted journey? He would not then be away from home and hearth. That is how the Sethia himself started out. Today he is able to rub shoulders with the gentry and he did not want that the person who was his minion should wear suit and boot, be his equal and sit at the same table.

> **Panjumal**: Wow, what a surprise! You told me the Sethia had no foresight. This speaks volumes!
> **Bherumal**: The Sethias only have time to plot and plan the destruction of others—more so their own community. They've been at it for two generations. What they cannot bear to think of is the well-being and betterment of their fellow beings.
> **Panjumal**: Is there some secret reason for the Sethias to encourage their employees to drink, even at a considerable loss to themselves?
> **Bherumal**: Certainly! All employees or partners working overseas are free to indulge in alcohol. The Sethia is aware of this and encourages them because his profits far exceed his losses. When these employees return home to Hyderabad, after a stipulated period, they have to spend their own money

Sindhwork and Sindhworkis • 233

on liquor. This way, they would perforce have to do job after job and can never get out of the Sethia's clutches. Were they not to drink, their minds would be clear and they would save so much more and start their businesses at home. They would understand the Sethia's underhanded ways and be intolerant and begin to demand their rights.

Panjumal: Bhai, forgive me, but I find it hard to believe that the Sethias could be selfish to such a great extent. I am sure this is just in your mind.

Bherumal: I admit, no one will readily accept what I have related to you. I also admit that the Sindhworkis themselves may never realize that they are, or were, living through such a phase. But reality cannot be denied. There are many who have lost the ability to think for themselves. They follow an unwritten law of bribing away workers from other firms, thus getting their own purpose served, and then discarding the workers like an old shoe. These secret practices are leading to the destruction of their own society and country. But what does it matter? Sindhwork is like a funfair. Each knows what the other is doing and must trample the other to get ahead.

To lend credibility to the above, I will give you an example. I hope it will clear your doubts.

A partner once had a lot of servants staying with him. During that time, there was a heavy duty on liquor, and so, it was very expensive. The Sethia thought that since it had become a custom to drink every day, if he discontinued the routine, the employees would rebel. So he devised a scheme. The liquor was costing him Rs 7–8 per person. He therefore announced that those who did not drink would get Rs 3 each. As a result, 25 per cent of the employees stopped drinking. After a few days 50 per cent had given it up. However, you will be shocked to know that when these men reached Hyderabad, and the time came for settling their accounts, the Sethia thought of the hole in his pocket, and declined to pay the employees their money. The manager, a wise and just person, told the Sethia he would lose good workers. So first the Sethia promised to give money to those who were willing to sign an agreement. Those who were not willing, or those who the Sethia was not willing to take on, were told to go home. Again, the manager intervened and advised the Sethia to honour his word or else those that he was taking back would never believe anything he said and would become disobedient. The Sethia complied and the rest were given their dues.

Now it was the turn of the teetotallers. They too demanded Rs 3 per month extra. But the Sethia simply refused, saying he could not be out of pocket for those on whom he did not spend on liquor in the first place. The result was that when new recruits were signed on, they started drinking (even though they were teetotallers and abhorred alcohol), and after a few days, told the manager that they would stop drinking if he added Rs 3 per month to their pay.

> **Panjumal:** Friend, I feel faint hearing all this. Would it be presumptuous of me to say that there must be a reason for the Sethias to open their homes for gambling?
>
> **Bherumal:** If you want to watch the fun, you should take the rounds of Sethia homes during *Shravan*, especially at the time of the Thadri festival, when card games are played. Stakes may begin at one anna but can skyrocket without limit. People who would not sign an agreement for less than Rs 100 per month beg to be taken on for Rs 80 or even less at this time. Although gambling goes on all year round, it reaches a peak during Thadri, when stakes are erratic and players become so reckless that they often end up penniless—or worse, in debt.

The Sethias do not consider gambling a vice. In fact, they often profit indirectly from the conversations and rivalries it sparks between employees and partners.

Panjumal: Bhai, enough! Forgive me! I do not have the strength to listen to any more of this. I did not even imagine that people could fall so low for the glitter of gold. I would consider it below my dignity to associate with such people.

So saying, Mr Panjumal walked away from the party.

The reader can evaluate the situation. The pheriewallahs were as much at fault as the Sethias, but it was the duty of the Sethias to discipline the pheriewallahs and keep them out of harm's way. As employers, they were also expected to be protectors.

As time passed, the Sethias made it a custom to give some money to those who were teetotallers and non-smokers. These sums were gradually increased so virtue would be on the rise and vice on the decline. The homes have since been closed to gambling. This was for the good of all the youngsters who were easily led to vice.

18 State of Sindhworki 'Servants'

I don't think there could be any Sindhworki who made money while working under the Sethias.

Most of them would return home only to immediately sign another agreement, on the strength of which they could borrow from the Sethia so they could take their holiday and rest in comfort. One starts to reflect as to why the Sindhworki employees are always broke even though their pay is not meagre; Rs 25 is their pocket money because all else is given to them by the Sethia. They incur no expense on boarding, lodging and transport. Many educated young men in Sindh would give their eye teeth for such remuneration. Why then are these Sindhworkis not able to better their lot?

I think the reasons for this downhill slide may be alcoholism, gambling and a lack of education, which makes them spend their savings carelessly on wine, women and song.

The Sindhworkis are not aware of business norms and sign agreements with no knowledge of their rights as they are not aware of the laws of the land. The Sethias, in turn, take full advantage of this and do everything that is illegal. None of the countries where the Sethias have businesses would allow such slavery. An agreement would have the same terms and conditions—be it for the first timer or the much-maligned manager drawing Rs 200 per month. The agreement states that the employee must go wherever the Sethia sends him and undertake whatever work he is asked to do. In short, he should be as meek as a goat led to a slaughterhouse. The reins of his life were given to the manager who, of course, was accountable only to the Sethia.

The agreement also specified how much the employee must remit home each month. His pay would start the day he set sail and would discontinue the moment he stopped working. He would not be paid for the time required for travel. If he discontinued work for any reason, he would have to pay for his own fare and, in addition, a further Rs 200, which would be the loss incurred for such termination of services. Also, the expenses of his lodge and board would be deducted on his arrival in Hyderabad.

Even a person with limited intelligence would realize that the agreement is favourable only, and I say only, to the Sethia. The employees, literally called 'servants', were treated as beasts of burden. The poor recruit had no choice but to comply. He was also expected to do the marketing, act as housekeeper and, at night, serve as the Sethia's masseur.

If the contracted period of work was two and a half years and the manager 'requested' (in reality, ordered) the employee to stay on for another five or six months, he had to comply. He was not told how much remuneration he would receive at the end of that period. The managers normally promised an enhanced pay, but at the journey's end, the Sethia typically declined to pay. What was the poor employee to do?

The Sethia would sign an agreement with the employee and in all probability not send him out for the next six months. Or there is every likelihood that at the end of six months he would be told that his services were not required, and the agreement stood cancelled. This meant a loss of valuable time and opportunity—time in which he could have joined another firm. Having borrowed money for survival over those six months, he was now in debt and left with two choices: either repay it in order to sign with another firm or beg like a dog for a job with the firm he could have joined. If per chance he was sent to a place where the climate was harmful to his health, half the contracted pay would be gone by way of medical fees and medicines. The Sethia absolved himself of any responsibility.

If he does not get a transfer to a place with a better climate, the employee has to foot all transport bills. The manager then decides what work to assign him. He may be asked to cook for the company, even do housework, i.e. sweeping and swabbing or other menial labour. In return, he will get a place to sleep and a simple meal, which could well mean dry bread and tea or, if the manager so chooses, a helping of pulao. No one dared complain for fear that he would have to pay return fare home plus Rs 200 for the loss of work.

If we were to relate all that the drunken managers did to the poor workers, it would make the reader's hair stand on end.

19 To Take Work Against Business Norms Does Not Bring About Much Profit

A loyal servant is one who considers his boss's work as his own. He is happy when his boss prospers and is sad when his boss suffers a loss. But the law of nature is that you can only feel for your boss if you are linked to him through business and you can feel the pinch of loss or the exhilaration of gain. Were the employee to get a commission on all sales, he would work hard to enhance the profits of the boss and delight in doing so—not otherwise.

With the Sethias, it is not so. The Sindhworki gets paid for the period of time he is away from home. There is no surety of bonus at the end of the contract. It is left entirely to the goodwill of the Sethias and their partners. A worker can only hope for this after a successful two-contract journey. By then he is well versed in the tricks of the trade. All the employee must do is follow the old adage: 'when in Rome, do as the Romans do'. The manager has to be pleased at all costs. His accounts are not to be reported because the Sethias themselves earn by illegal means and do not want to hear anything as long as the profits keep coming in. So they follow the lesson taught of the three wise monkeys: 'See no evil, hear no evil, speak no evil.' The employee then returns home with respect and his pockets full of gold.

Some servants work diligently and present themselves for work every day. Others feign headaches or stomach aches and skip work for five or six days a month. Yet both get the same pay. Managers of smaller branches also get the same pay as those managing the larger branches without discrimination, even though one branch manager hands over Rs 10,000 and the other only Rs 2,000. Since the Sethias show no appreciation for the hard-working, honest employee, on subsequent journeys, the managers who showed higher profits start pilfering and feathering their own nests.

After maybe three or four such contracted journeys, the salesman matures from a teenager into a young man and then begins to play games with the Sethias. They ask for partnerships and become managers of the firm. They have access to the books and learn the tricks of the trade, making contacts with other firms and sometimes getting the better of the Sethias.

This is why most Sindhworkis become dishonest. But if that is the case, how is it that the Sethias still offer them partnerships? They choose those who pilfer discreetly and do not show off. Those who give the Sethias a marginally higher profit than their colleagues or curry favour by telling tales about their colleagues, and thus become the Sethia's favourite and rise to the much envied position of partner.

20. Who Is a Sindhworki Thief?

Sindhworkis are often accused of being dishonest. But, as the saying goes, you are only a thief if you are caught.

The Sethias and their managers are always on the lookout for such persons, and will never re-employ anyone who is caught pilfering.

Some employees either transfer money to their families through private sources or smuggle it on their person on their return home or send parcels from abroad using goods taken from the Sethia's stock to his family. Those who pilfer and squander the money wherever they are working are often excused. Not openly, but the Sethia will turn a Nelson's eye to such thefts. Moreover, they have no proof in hand. When these cunning salesmen reach home, their pockets are empty and it is only then that the Sethia settles their accounts. But how can it be proven that they pilfered, when they have not a paaee in hand?

21 The Behaviour of Servants

The bosses cannot expect their servants' loyalty when they treat them badly. The servants know what is laid down in the agreement, i.e. the remuneration due to them will definitely be given to them. It is the other terms of the agreement that they seek to balance. The only way they can do this is by taking an advance on their monies. They take a large sum of money before they embark on their contracted journey. The Sethia, anxious to recruit staff, thinks, *Why not give them with a large heart and show my magnanimity? At the end of the contract I'll find a way of squeezing out their lifeblood.* At the end of the contractual period, the Sethia often finds that the servant owes him Rs 50–55. The servant then plays a cat-and-mouse game to collect his favours, and the Sethia has no option but to give in to get his money back.

Here in Hyderabad, recruits who look simple and poor, and who are ready to do the Sethia's bidding, often turn out to be rascals. Only once the agreement is signed and a substantial amount of money taken by way of an advance do they start for their place of work. The manager finds that getting work out of them takes much longer. The servants get into arguments and do not hesitate to snub the managers. The partners find themselves in a quandary. If they sack the employee, they will have to pay his return fare. He has already taken an advance of Rs 200–400 and the fare already spent would be Rs 200–300. Also, as much would have been spent on his boarding and lodging. Over and above that, they would have to look for another employee and spend as much on him. So the managers are forced to pamper these rascals and extract whatever work

Sindhwork and Sindhworkis • 243

they can. There are not many who are so rotten, but one rotten apple spoils the whole basket. Similarly, one rotten worker in the factory can cause a lot of problems. At least 10 per cent to 20 per cent of such undesirable persons cross the Sethia's path.

Let it not be understood that such people are starving on the streets—not at all! The moment another firm comes to know that this scruffy fellow has left Mr A and pulled him down a notch, Mr B will delight in the loss of Mr A and employ the rascal at an enhanced pay—be it a Rs 10 or Rs 20 increment.

There is no understanding among the Sindhworkis that employment should be granted only after seeing a leaving certificate. In many instances, a servant signs greements with two firms, takes advantage of both, and then joins a third firm. And off he goes before one can say Jack Robinson! So, for the price of one, he takes three advances and becomes a rich man even before the commencement of his journey. In a community where such unscrupulous practices exist and no one takes any notice of it, how can one hope its youth will be virtuous?

 Why Do They Employ Local Staff?

The question arises: if Sindhworki salesmen turn out to be rotters, why don't the Sethias employ local staff? All expenses amount to Rs 50–100 per person, at least (in times of war, the fare itself can be as high as Rs 1,500). However, local workers are not considered suitable for the Sindhworki business. They will not be party to the underhand ways of the Sindhworki businessmen. They believe in self-help and honesty of purpose. If it is a 'nine to five' job, it cannot be stretched to 'nine to nine'.

The Hyderabad Bhaiband lads are used to the strange schedules of the Sethias, hence it is advisable to employ their own kind, who understand and accept the 'slave situation' that has existed since time immemorial. Their ancestors did it. So they do the same and accept the ancient ways. 'Moving with the times' is, it seems, an axiom reserved only for the Western world.

 Lack of Proper Accounts Gives the Servants an Opportunity to Slacken, and Then to Vice

In the modern age, when accounting has become easy, even the least knowledgeable of businessmen can balance their accounts. Not so the Sindhworki!

Each year, they open their books and their eyes to examine profit and loss. If the books show profit, they would just shut them without a second glance to consider if the profits could have been much more and, if so, how they could rectify their mistakes or pull up the managers. For the Sethias, the aura of profit is enough to move forward to another year of business. Staff are engaged haphazardly. Goods are not price-tagged. If salesmen are told not to sell any item for, say, less than Rs 5 each, and if a salesman is a glib-talker, and can sell the item for Rs 10, he makes an entry of Rs 8 and pockets the remaining Rs 2. The Sethia is happy that he made Rs 3, which was more than the expected price, and the salesman is happy that he pulled the wool over his boss's eyes and gained Rs 2 on the sly.

Stock-taking is unheard of, or rather, it is considered ominous. It is like the age-old adage 'if you count money, it slips through your fingers'. So the Sethias also believed that as long as profits keep losses at bay, keeping stock books is not necessary. The extras would be considered a windfall and squandered away.

I am sure that if they were to be taught to keep books of stock, and take a little time off from other activities to understand the system, the Sethias would be able to prevent unnecessary expenditure. At the same time, the employees would be on their best behaviour, knowing full well that if a surprise inspection of stocks would be conducted, they could be caught, branded as thieves and left jobless for the rest of their lives. Not only that, they would be social outcastes!

24 Sindhworki Partners

A Sindhworki is eligible for partnership after completing three or four journeys (a journey could comprise between 2½ and 3½ years of work experience). At such a time, the pay scale would move from Rs 25 to somewhere between Rs 150 and Rs 200.

There are many classes of partnerships. Some involve one, two or even three partners who oversee one shop and share equally in the profits and losses with the Sethias. There could be three or four such assignments in different cities involving 5–8 partners, but again, the Sethia gets 50 per cent of profits and the remaining is shared by the partners.

The third kind is called an ordinary partnership. This entitles the partner to anywhere between 1 per cent and 8 per cent of the profits—the rest is the Sethia's. The thought seldom strikes the partners that the Sethias are always on the winning side. For instance, the Sethia gets 50 per cent share, and if he has four brothers, they are also included as partners, as are the ordinary partners from other families. As a family grows, new members are added as partners and are allocated a share of the profits, irrespective of whether they work in the firm or not. In short, family members become sleeping partners.

The agreement/contract for partnership is a journey of 5–10 years. After working oversees for 2½ years, a partner can return home to rest for 6 months to 1½ years with all expenses paid. His remuneration during this period could be between Rs 200 and Rs 1,000 per month.

There is a saying, 'You can fool some of the people some of the time. You can fool some of the people all of the time. But you cannot fool all of the people all of the time.' Yet the Sethias are the only breed who are successful in fooling all the people all the time!

25 Agreements/Contracts for Partnership

When the system of 'partnership' was first introduced, the employees/servants thought a great favour had been bestowed upon them. They did not have the courage to question their Sethias about the terms and conditions of the agreement. They were naïve enough to accept the Sethia's goodwill, sweet talk and verbal promises. It was only much later, when partners were deceived and their rightful dues not paid, that they realized everything should have been put down in black and white.

Even so, many of the Sethias who were considered upright and honest within the community (I will not name them) resorted to cheating by drawing up an agreement at the insistence of the partner but not signing it. The partner would be asked to take charge of the office and told, 'We will sign it and send it to you', but the agreement never arrived. The partner, who was happy with the promotion, soon found himself back to square one, where his remuneration and work conditions were at the mercy of the Sethia! The Sethia then reasoned that the investment and industry were his, and that the working partner should be content with receiving just enough to lead a comfortable life. He should not receive so much that the partner could accumulate wealth, rise in stature and rub shoulders with him, the Sethia!

Some Sethias showed their authority and squashed the demands for a proper agreement. Those who had previously suffered for lack of signed documents insisted that they would not take on any assignments without a formal agreement. But the Sethias were always one step ahead. They would put pen to paper but the rules and regulations were of their own making—with double meanings. The partners prospered only up to the time they were required by the Sethia. The moment they had served their purpose or declined to extend their work period, the Sethia would drop the concerned employee like a hot brick and give him, the partner, only what the Sethia willed. The agreement was a farce and the partner had no evidence to appeal in a court of law.

 Partner Gains 40 Per Cent (6 Annas out of a Rupee) but Pays 50 Per Cent (8 Annas out of a Rupee) by Way of Loss

Who would believe that a partner could be so foolish as to take on such an agreement. But I shall prove to you the truth of the chapter title. If the partner in charge of the factory has a 50:50 entitlement to the gains alongside the Sethia, he is also held equally responsible for any losses. In case there is a loss, not only must he bear 50 per cent of it, but even his earnings from twelve months of working partnership may be confiscated. This brings down his percentage of gain. The loss is actually paid out of company accounts so the Sethia invariably profits while the partner is always at a loss.

However, God's grace is on the Sindhworkis and such situations of massive losses are rare. Since partners keep on getting some pocket money, no one has bothered to really look into the finer points of the agreements.

Partnership Agreements Are Redundant

The Sethias take no notice of any Sindhwork partner if his monthly earnings are Rs 100–200. But God forbid if, by hard work, the earnings of the partner rises to Rs 500–1,000 per month, the Sethia would become agitated, and plot and plan how to back out of giving the partner so much money. Conscience would mean nothing to him. He would shamelessly try to cheat the partner out of his dues, come hell or high water.

One should not forget that a partnership is offered only after 12–14 years of service. By then, the young man has given the best years of his life to the company. He may now be a married man, and apart from supporting his own family he has the responsibility of ageing parents and younger siblings. The Sethia will not stop to think that the man may be in poor health and need all his savings. The glitter of gold blinds the Sethia and his only thought is how to prevent the money from slipping through his fingers. Whether it is rightfully his or not matters little.

By and large, there would have been no proper agreement. The partner is still dependent on the Sethia for his monthly pay. Were he to go to court, even his regular income would stop. He would also have overheads of the lawyer's fees. At any given point the Sethia would be able to buy off the partner's lawyers as the cost would be a drop in the ocean for him. Ultimately, the wretched partner keeps quiet and has to be satisfied with the crumbs that fall off his master's table.

28 Injustices Against the Sindhworkis

Oral statements by Sindhworkis:

EXAMPLE 1

I was sent overseas for Sindhwork for a remuneration of Rs 35 per month. Initially I was contracted for two journeys, and when I joined for a third contract, my pay was a total of Rs 60 per month.

I was allotted work on the outskirts of the city. Then the Sethias transferred me to their factory. The factory manager told me that there was a town some distance away from the factory where one could do roaring business. A new city, a new language, unknown people! I was a little reticent. The manager offered me a share of 40 per cent to 60 per cent of all goods sold there. I took courage and went to that town. It would be a waste of the reader's time to relate the difficulties I experienced there. But the carrot before the donkey was the 40 per cent I was promised and, somehow or the other, I managed to set up a business.

The goods required would be sent from the factory, for which I charged a 10 per cent commission. Had I sent for the goods from Bombay through the Sethias I would have got 20 per cent, but that would have been time-consuming. As I was the local partner, I did not mind giving up part of the earnings to my colleagues.

I worked for three years. When I returned home, I calculated that my net earnings should be at least Rs 50,000, after giving the Sethia Rs 1,20,000. I was a poor man. Returning with Rs 50,000 in hand—you can well imagine my joy. I was returning home like gentry. Thirty years ago, this was a princely sum (this story was disclosed in 1920) and very few could boast of a capital of Rs 50,000. On landing in Bombay, the Sethias welcomed me with open arms. They showered expensive gifts upon me, which usually only their partners were entitled to receive.

In Hyderabad, I rested for 2–3 months. I started looking for a plot of land where I could build a house. Every plot or bungalow I saw and approved, the Sethias would create a snag. Four months went by and the house seemed like a mirage. The Sethias disapproved of one and all. Every month, I was paid my salary and, in addition, was given Rs 700–800 to make ornaments for my family.

Eventually, the time came for me to return to work. Every time I told them to settle my accounts, they would make some excuse. Ultimately, the Sethias said, 'Do not worry about the accounts, when you return for your next journey, we will settle everything. If you need some money now, we will advance it to you, but you must sign the agreement.' I smelt a rat. I told the Sethia, 'I will return only when you clear my account.' Bhai was furious and asked me to return the next day to clear my accounts.

The clerk was sent for. He showed me the books. I had been paid only Rs 60 per month. Nothing of the local partnership was forthcoming, nor was my commission paid to me. To top it all, the monies paid to me as gratis during my rest period, and the gifts they had given me as goodwill, had all been deducted, and now I owed the Sethia Rs 2,000! I thought I was dreaming until the Sethia's booming voice brought me back to the present, 'Young man, if you don't return the Rs 2,000 due to us within three days, I will file a suit against you!'

I have no recollection of how I reached home. I later

learnt that I had been unconscious for three days. I had a high fever and was bedridden for twenty days. I could think of nothing except the loan I had to return and how I had been tricked into a fake partnership, and how I was pushed into raising my standards of living for which I will suffer penury for the rest of my life!

Some days later, the Sethia's brother came to me and encouraged me to have a dialogue with the senior Sethia. In the end, I was offered a legal partnership and the Rs 2,000 was written off as a bonus for the start of the journey. Having had a bad experience, I was not very enthusiastic, but rather became very cautious in business. Every month, the profit would be around Rs 200–300, enough for me to live comfortably.

I worked thus for twenty years. No one complained as they were getting sufficient income. But I could not really save. The thought occurred to me, 'What of my old age?' I might be able to work for another couple of contracted periods, say, about six years. I strove to do better, get more commissions, as well as amass quite some wealth for the Sethias. After those six years, when I returned home, I told the Bhais that I was an old man and didn't have the strength to work any more. So would they be kind enough to grant me a pension and give me my *lungi-poti*?

The Sethias thought, 'Now we can dispense with him, but how do we deprive him of his dues?' So every day, they sang a new song and made excuses, 'Mister, the goods you left behind, some may be old or damaged. What of those?' I replied, 'Gracious Bhai, you know that damaged or discarded goods are written off lower than the cost price at the end of the contract.' Bhai said, 'That is not our custom. That percentage will have to be deducted from your account.'

I felt I was being cheated out of my bonus, but hopefully he would give me my dues for the work done. I did some mental arithmetic and thought, *Okay, he is going to take away Rs 5,000 or Rs 10,000 against damaged goods—some 8 per cent to 10 per cent of my money. It doesn't matter. I have no option anyway*. A few days later, the Bhai called me and asked, 'Do you think, if we sell the factory, it would cover the cost of damages that you have recorded in the books?' I replied, 'The duty in that town is pretty heavy.' 'That is true,' he then said, 'then we must have clear accounts.' I realized that he had put me in a spot. Were he to deduct duties and damages and the goods left behind, and sell the factory on which duty had to be paid, I would lose my bonus, my work money and pension. He had so manoeuvred the situation that all expenses were to be paid by me. The Sethia had not only pulled the rug from under my feet, but he had also blown the roof over my head. I prayed to the Almighty to let me die with dignity.

The next day, I again went to the Bhai and said, 'My gracious lord, if you desire to sell the factory so that you don't undergo any loss, allow me to go and clinch the deal for you. Maybe I will be able to get you a premium of Rs 5,000 or Rs 10,000.' Bhai was furious. He went red in the face and showered me with abuses. He said, 'All right, do that. Add to it the advances you have been paid. Also the salary deductions and your share of the losses on damaged goods—and then bring us the money! You have nothing to do with the shop—that is ours to do as we like.'

Dear readers, consider the cunning! A factory to be sold at my loss, but the shop and showroom of thirty years standing was theirs. Were the showroom devoid of goods and empty as a tomb, it would still fetch them a 'goodwill' of Rs 20,000! I was just dumbstruck.

Some friends advised me to take legal action, but I refused. I knew of another partner who had been deprived of Rs 10,000–15,000 by his Sethias. He spent Rs 1,50,000 on the case, but the Sethias were of a stronger breed, and therefore he lost both the Rs 10,000, which were his rightful dues, and the Rs 1,50,000 on the advocates and court fees. Since that day, no partner has ever dared to oppose any Sethia. I was not about to be the next fool.

After much deliberation, I went to the boss and, on bended

knees and with folded hands, I requested the respected Bhai to consider my age and the years I spent in their service. He smirked and said, 'You have to pay me Rs 2,000.' I signed on a stamp paper that I would pay them Rs 2,000. I did find the courage to tell them as a parting shot that I would pay the Rs 2,000 only if they filed a suit against me! I knew fully well that they would not do that. A person who had served them loyally for 30 years had a certain status in society and the Sethia's name would be mud were he to file a suit against such a person.

Dear readers, I would gladly disclose my name but for fear of the Sethia's anger and evil ways, which would land me in deeper trouble. Thus I conclude my personal experience.

EXAMPLE 2

I was a working partner in a Sethia's subsidiary factory. Every month, I used to save Rs 50–70. I worked there for four years. There was no written agreement of any kind. Every year, there were sufficient profits out of which my share was 30 per cent to 40 per cent. The Lord showered his blessings upon me and that year trade in the city went up by leaps and bounds. The more goods I ordered, the more I sold and the more the manager fleeced customers. I did not pay much attention as I was making enough and adopted a 'live and let live' policy.

Eventually, the time came when Bhai refused to supply goods. He did not want me to prosper. If I did well, his share would be way beyond mine, but it also smelt of my success and that he did not relish. I appealed to him that if he did not want to be my supplier, he should allow me to get the goods from other sources. He refused point blank, saying that was not their system. All goods must be purchased from them. At last he agreed to supply me with goods at the price he sold to his retail customers, sometimes even more.

Still, fortune favoured me and I was able to sell all the goods at an enhanced price. The manager was at his journey's end and I too was due to go home. I thought it a good idea to let the manager keep the accounts together with mine. I got the shock of my life when I saw the accounts—items for which I had paid Rs 10 each, the manager put down as Rs 6, and sometimes even Rs 5. When I protested, he said those were their rules—as some of the goods had become old and outdated. I kept quiet and thought that on reaching Hyderabad I would entreat the gracious Sethia to do justice. After all, even with the manager's falsified accounts, I still had Rs 30,000 due, and I hoped for more if the Sethia was just and ruled in my favour.

With great joy I arrived in Hyderabad, to my country, my family, my home. After a few days, I went to meet the Sethia and requested an advance on my account. I needed Rs 1,000 to perform my son's thread ceremony. Bhai said to 'come back tomorrow'. The next day, again it was 'tomorrow', and so it went, but the 'tomorrow' never came. Eventually, I pawned some family jewellery and performed the thread ceremony.

When I had reached the end of my resources, I once again appealed to the Bhai, and alternated my request with the manager, asking them to please clear my account. Two months went by. Then came the day of reckoning. The revered Sethia sat like a sombre judge. The manager became the plaintiff, and I the aggrieved was made defendant. All this was prearranged and stage-managed, pre-planned.

Plaintiff: 'Bhai, at face value, the accounts show a profit, but some items that should be on the credit side, if your revered self so judges, will not show profit, i.e. the goods that I have itemized and left behind. According to our rules, 10 per cent of their value should go to your fund, which remains outstanding from the junior partner. Secondly, the interest on the purchase of the factory has also not been credited to you. Thirdly, on his say so, goods were sent for from other working partners. They are collecting dust and the percentage of their value should also go to your account. Fourth, he imported goods worth Rs 60,000–

70,000 from other sources on which we could have earned 6.5 per cent commission. So that should come to us. Fifth, other factory workers will now demand bonuses, so a share of his profits should be deducted for that charitable fund.'

Hearing all this, I broke down in tears and said, 'Gracious Sethia, you are the judge here. You have to be fair. The manager was with me before we set sail and he did not inform me of all that he is putting down in front of you.' The Sethia replied coldly, 'I shall reflect on this and inform you.' But until the verdict was pronounced, I was dying a thousand deaths! I entreated that I be given some cash as creditors were hounding me. The magnanimous Bhai declared I should be given Rs 500.

Several weeks went by and there was no news. Ultimately, I went to the Sethia again. He called the clerk and said, 'Attend to this poor fellow's accounts.' The manager put a lot of hitches and said he would not be able to face all this. 'But let us sit down and sort out the mess.' I thought the Sethia was going to be fair—but it was not to be. He told the clerk to write Rs 6,000 for the goods received, Rs 5,000 for the goods left behind and Rs 3,000 by way of interest on said goods. He also told him to add to it Rs 5,000 by way of the commission I deprived them of on the goods I purchased there (Rs 4,000 was the amount but bring it to Rs 5,000 for the fund of the bonuses to the workers). Now he told the clerk to total the whole thing. The clerk quickly ran his fingers down the column and declared that only Rs 600 was due to me.

Tears rolled down my face in rivulets. I pleaded and reasoned, but to no avail. As a show of magnanimity on the part of the gracious Sethia, in a booming voice, he ordered the clerk to 'give this hard-working fellow a bonus of Rs 1,000'. My insides seethed with anger and frustration at the injustice meted out to me. I returned home with Rs 1,600 in my pocket and distributed it amongst my debtors. My homecoming had soured. The hard work of four years and the hard-earned money was nowhere in sight. I was again the poorest of the poor, with only dreams for company.

EXAMPLE 3

In 1912, I left my old firm and switched jobs. My condition was that when the new factory/firm started, I would be made a partner. There was already a partner in the firm and his deal was '40 cents to the dollar were his and 60 cents to the dollar were the Sethia's'. The system was that partners received 50 per cent and Sethias 50 per cent. It was not clearly stated what my share would be—and it was not the done thing to bargain with the Sethias, who were renowned both at home and abroad.

The Sethia was paying my household expenses. From time to time he gave his word about the job and after eight months the previous partner returned home. I took over charge and the business prospered. When the partner came back, I went home. I stayed in Hyderabad for one and a half years, but not once did I enquire as to the terms of my partnership. I felt it did not seem right to question the bosses, and believed they would give me what was due. Whatever I wanted during my stay in Hyderabad was provided to me so I had no reason to doubt the Sethia's integrity.

After 18 months, I returned to work and the other partner again went home to rest. The profits that started out with $5,000–8,000 per annum boomed to $30,000–35,000 per annum during the period of my partnership. It was a good trading period. The rate of the dollar at that time fluctuated between Rs 1.25 and Rs 1.50. I worked for a further period of two years. The previous partner did not return and the Sethia sent another man who carefully took over the accounts.

I collected the balance sheets for 1916 (having worked since 1912) and returned home to Hyderabad. There I learnt that my previous partner had become mentally unwell. Upon further enquiry, I learned that the man had taken on some trade in

Hyderabad. Even though the time given to us was called 'rest time' how could any man remain idle for 1½–2 years? The Sethia was very angry and called him and, in front of a large gathering, slapped the manager. The man could not take this insult and suffered a breakdown. When I met him, he was all right and said that he had worked with the Sethia for thirty years and according to the paperwork his share should be Rs 60,000–70,000. He had not even got to asking for that. Only a paltry sum of Rs 2,000–4,000 was paid, and he was insulted before so many people known to him.

This meant that the Sethia had no intention of giving him his money, and was slyly slipping out of the deal. When he became his normal self again, he took charge of the situation and humbly pleaded with the Sethia to clear his accounts. The Sethia would not budge an inch. He stood firm as the Rock of Gibraltar and, apart from clearing accounts and giving his dues, he stopped the man's monthly remuneration. He knew all was lost. He went from pillar to post and asked other Sethias to intervene. At last his boss said, 'Let him give me a signed statement that my decision will be acceptable to him, and I will set about clearing his accounts.' But, he said to me, 'How could I trust a person with my life? He had already pushed me nearly into the madhouse. How could I trust such a person? When all doors were shut, I debated appealing in the court. But I knew that if I could not get what was rightfully mine from the Sethia, could he not sway the court with his millions and put me in the poorhouse?' Poor man. Worried for his wife and children's future, the man's health deteriorated further, and he eventually died, saying, 'What I earned for my family, these rascal Sethias have stolen.'

Seeing the distress of his wife and children at the funeral, I thought, *Surely the Sethias will give them something.* The dying man kept repeating that the Sethias had done him out of so many thousands and, to top it all, said that he owed them a few hundred. I knew the widow would not be able to fight the court case and would ultimately fall on the charity of the Sethias.

I do not want to be the judge of who was right and who was wrong, but this made me sit up and think and secure my own position. I did some mental arithmetic, and realized that the Sethias had to give me Rs 25,000–30,000. I requested an advance of Rs 1,000. Some excuse was given. I insisted. They refused point blank. I took courage and said, 'When we are not sure of getting money for our own hard work, then I think we should part peacefully. I do not want to take another journey. So please clear my accounts.'

Lady luck was on my side. The Sethia had to show the accounting and percentages of the partners in the court for the previous partner. Accordingly the dead partner's percentage was 24 cents to the dollar and 20 cents to the dollar was my share. The Sethia's share was 56 cents to the dollar. I demanded that I be given equal share and also be paid for the time I stayed in Hyderabad (Sindh). The Sethia replied, 'You will be paid only up to the time you left the factory, and at the rate of Rs 1.50 to the dollar.'

Our factory was in Hong Kong and the system was that after deducting the exchange rate, payments were made in Hong Kong dollars. Whatever the current rate, we would be given the rupee value, either in hand or kept on file. By and large, the Hong Kong dollar was equal to Rs 1.25–1.35 and sometimes went up to Rs 1.50. But currently the price of silver had shot up, and so had the dollar price. It was now fetching Rs 2 to Rs 2.35.

For the last few years the factory had been doing very well and the exchange rate had climbed. Seeing the situation, the Sethias thought they would have to fork out quite a lot. So to save a few thousands, they said, 'We will give you money at the exchange rate of Rs 1.50 to the dollar, and no more. Go do your damnedest!' I moved heaven and earth, sought advice of all and sundry, but failing all, resorted to the justice of the law.

Bhai decided to drag the court case and swore that the files had not been sent from Hong Kong. I knew for a fact that the files were here in Hyderabad. I had brought them myself. I was flabbergasted—how could such famed and named persons take a false oath against their less privileged employees? Who, indeed, is one to trust?

29 A Critical Analysis

Hopefully the reader can evaluate the treatment meted out by the Sethias to their partners. It was even worse for the ordinary worker, the salesman. They reposed their faith and trust in their bosses, worked themselves to the bone, and yet, when death came, they died as paupers. Pursuing justice through the courts without a steady income is impossible. The Sethias are well aware that their junior partners are financially incapable of competing with them. A court case might drag on for 5–7 years. How is the poor man to feed his family? The Sethias were so used to perpetuating injustice and became so fearless of courts that they did not hesitate to belittle the *mukhiyas* or *panchas,* the heads of the community, who tried to mediate and bring about a settlement to avoid court proceedings.

I am certain that many partners' families must be in the poorhouse. The Sethias grab what is rightfully their partners' and live in luxury at their cost. They feel that they can purchase even God with their money. Perhaps this is one reason why they give lavishly to religious institutions—to salve their conscience.

According to our religion, if we believe there is a God above, His mill may grind slowly, but surely. And for people like the Sethias, the good Lord will have to create a hell even worse than the one that already exists.

 # The Outcome

Every partner feels that he does not get what he deserves. At no time does he possess sufficient capital to start his own business. If he had, he would not tolerate the Sethia and would not stay in his employment even a day longer than necessary.

On the one hand, the Sethias plot and plan how best to deprive their partners of their dues and delay settlement of accounts. On the other hand, the partners try to take the maximum possible advance from the Sethias, as they know well they would likely be cheated in the final rechecking, especially if business has been booming and profits have been high. So the tug of war goes on and the fragmentation of capital allows no opening for a business for the partners.

The Sindhwork system continues to operate in the footsteps of the ancestors. If an experienced senior partner tries to modernize, the Sethia makes life miserable for him and eventually sacks him. Experience without capital puts him back in square one, so he sticks to the traditional ways where there is no chance of failure. In spite of this, Sindhwork has prospered a hundredfold, so life goes on in the same old manner.

Lack of Education Is the Cause of the Faulty System

I have mentioned in previous chapters the reasons why the Sindhworki Bhaiband community has remain unlettered. From times gone by until today, the Bhaiband community has not been given a sound educational foundation. One has to dig deep to understand why they cut out education from their lives. One feels sorry for the Bhaiband community's decline.

Had the community been educated, not only Hyderabad, Sindh and the Provinces, but the whole of Hindustan would have profited. Business acumen coupled with education and sound values would have been a march forward. It is this Sindhworki community that is spread all over the world and has business houses in every major city. There is not a language that one or the other Sindhworki does not speak fluently like a native. Having had the dunce cap put on their heads for their lack of education, apart from business, they have not cared to find out where the world has reached. In these last thirty or forty years, Japan has reached its zenith of power. Europe is running towards a certain goal of advancement. But these people cannot see beyond the tips of their noses.

Sindhworkis hold their heads high and blow their own trumpets in front of the Amil and Bhaiband communities in Hyderabad. While the world has made extraordinary progress in the past fifty years, these handful—nay, just five to eight—of Sindhworkis who became lakhpatis sing their own praises. They would do better to reflect with humility.

We will be justified in blaming the lack of education among the Sindhworkis for the decline and lack of progress in our country. They are the real culprits.

32 Sindhworkis Are Traitors

The gold earned through the sweat-of-the-brow toil of a Sethia's working partners was swallowed up by the Sethias, while their partners' children starved. One cannot expect such people to be patriotic. Their conscience did not question, 'What have you done for your country or countrymen?'

In the olden days, the Sindhworkis patronized those goods made only by Sindhi craftsmen, and later, by Hindustani craftsmen. As trade increased, they sold their goods in foreign lands and made large profits. Gradually, the foreigner traders drew them into their inner circle and had them sell local goods. Sometimes, they would even supply the Sindhworkis with their own patterns and have them supply according to their requirements. The Sindhworkis found this convenient, as transactions could be completed immediately. There was no waiting period for the goods to come from Sindh and costs of clearing and transportation were also saved, so the profit margin was higher. That was all right because, after all, the extra money earned was coming back to their homes. The crux of the question was, 'Why should Hindustani craftsmen suffer while the foreign craftsmen prospered?'

Previously, the Sindhworki shops overflowed with Indian goods. Now 95 per cent of the goods are from Japan and Europe. A measly 5 per cent is Indian, which was thrown in a corner to collect dust, too shameful to be displayed before any customer. Foreign contracts made them export 99 per cent of their goods in return for 1 per cent of Indian goods. Other countries even tried to copy Hindustani goods but were unsuccessful in making them.

Sindhworkis would not have hesitated to order consignments from them.

You have read in previous chapters how shabbily the Sethias treated their poor, innocent countrymen. So if they become traitors to their own country, what does it matter and what can one expect of them?

33 'Desh Hateshta' or 'Uncaring of Your Own': What Kind of Bird Is That?

History records that, since time immemorial, Sindhworkis have cared neither for their countrymen nor for their country. Their name, Sindhworki, should be reminder enough for them. They became Sethias because of the beautiful craftsmanship of Sindhi goods, which fetched them immense wealth in foreign markets. They used to give thousands of rupees in advance to the craftsmen but always fell short of the supply as the goods sold quicker than they could be produced.

So the Sindhworkis had to look elsewhere. The workmanship of Sindh was par excellence and the goods supplied were of high quality. When quality gave way to quantity, one could not say, but fewer orders were placed with Sindhi artisans. For example, Sindh was famous for its real zardozi embroidery, made with genuine gold and silver threads. Some craftsmen in Madras started making the same embroidery using imitation metal threads, so the cost came down. The Sindhworkis started patronizing the Madras craftsmen who turned out more and more quantity, but at the expense of quality, employing anyone who could just stitch. The result was the decline of the craft in Sindh.

If the Sindhworkis had spared even one thought for their own people, they could have relocated the gifted craftsmen to Madras, given them the required patterns and cloth, and told them to use imitation threads. But to save a few extra thousand rupees, they held their work-in-trade brethren to ransom. Some Sindhworkis may smirk and say we buy the *bochhan* from Sindh, but that was not such a great deal. The ladies who embroidered these scarves did it out of love, as a hobby. They did not care to sell them but perhaps to add to their daughters' trousseau. Now it is a dying art—those ladies are no more. Many have now sold those scarves as art pieces and in the years to come one may not even find a single such piece to feast one's eyes on.

Even now it is not too late. The Sethias could well get the cloth, patterns and threads aligned with the fashion trends of other countries and give it to the women in their own homes to embroider. Initially they should pay them a good price so that the women feel it worth their while. As word spreads, more and more women will desire that extra income and will put their hands to work for longer hours. Once the supply far exceeds the demand, automatically the price will fall to an affordable level. This way, many lower-middle-class Sindhi women will augment their family income and keep themselves occupied and out of mischief and gossip.

Firms that have businesses abroad order goods from foreign craftsmen and sell those goods in Sindh. Indirectly they, the Sindhworkis, are helping the foreign craftsmen to prosper. Why can't they use their heads and work out a system where they can help Sindhi craftsmen to thrive too? They could take a few of them abroad, show them the styles of those countries and perhaps teach them the popular stitching techniques there. They could return to Sindh to work with junior craftsmen on a larger scale, and export the products to foreign lands. This way, the wealth of Sindh will remain in Sindh. If the province prospers, the country will succeed in its march towards progress.

Foreigners are all the time thinking of ways to enrich their own countries and literally lure Sindhworkis with their glib talk. The Sindhworkis are easy prey and fall into their trap. They don't think twice about the loss to their own motherland. They come to Hyderabad only to rest and wallow in their wealth. Their days are spent in wine, women and song. Not a moment's thought is given to the upliftment of the Bhaiband community. Their minds run on how to be considered the big boss of the community who can do no wrong! If they lack virtues, how can one expect their junior partners or 'servants' to be virtuous? They are encouraged by the Sethias to indulge in drinking and gambling so that their minds are always bogged down and their pockets empty. It is easy to persuade such staff to take on journey after journey so they cannot start their own businesses.

 Lack of Humanity in Sindhwork Sethias

When the Bhaiband community reads the statements in this chapter, they may well sit up and think, *Are we really such fools that what we consider rest and leisure is actually a sacrifice of our precious lives at the altar of vice?* I am only presenting the facts and the reader can draw their own conclusions.

In a certain city, two Sindhworkis had their showrooms. The staff at these showrooms were perennially sick and kept losing weight. Some came back home to Hyderabad and died, while others died there within a very short time of their employment. When the cases were investigated, it was found that the shops were located in dead-end alleys where there was no air or sunlight. The area was swampy and the shops damp. The servants were never allowed out of the shop. When they shut these shops, they were required to sweat out the remaining hours in larger business houses of the Sethias. They were allowed very few hours of rest; as a result, they generally became victims of tuberculosis or other lung diseases and, at a very young age, took leave of this world to meet their forefathers.

One of the managers, after losing a few employees to 'Mr Death', decided to change the premises. But what of the young men who died in his employment? Did their family/heirs get any compensation? No, not at all! The young men were destined to die in such a way—how could the Sethia be blamed for their ill health or death? Maybe it was in their genes!

The second Sethia still has a shop in a similar alley. He does not care to change the premises or improve the lot of the employees by giving them proper diet and medication. Nor does he allow them free time to get fresh air. Some of the Hyderabad Sethias have factories in West Africa, situated on the seashore in tidal-prone, extremely humid areas. It is said of this land that it is a graveyard of foreigners—referring to the Sindhis. Whoever has gone there, only 20 per cent have been able to survive the vagaries of the harsh climate. Up to now about 50 persons have either died there or come home to Hyderabad in such poor health that they eventually died there.

These business houses exist even today, attracting new recruits who are ensnared by the glitter of gold. Unaware of the awful conditions of the place, nor that death is stalking them and that they can barely bring back even brass, let alone gold! Can the Sethias not open factories in better climes? Should they not place the facts before the recruits? Even a lesser person would be distressed to see the condition of the families of these young men and hear the wailing of the young widows. But the Sethias are made of hard metal and all they care about is money in their own pockets.

At one time a partner recruited the Sethia's relative to work at a factory in West Africa. The young man had already set sail. When the Sethia came to know about it, he sent telegrams at every port for that particular young man to disembark and return home. How is it that the Sethia did not leave it to destiny? Is destiny only for the poor and destitute, whose lifeblood is to be sucked out, but not for his own relatives?

Is there no *mukhiya*, *chaudhary* or headman of the community who will question the Sethia and persuade him to compensate the families of the men who died in his service?

These families are not even aware that their sons, husbands, brothers died to fulfil the insatiable lust for money of their 'gracious' lord and master.

 Inherent Drawbacks of Sindhworkis

We have already touched upon the subject of the lack of education among the Bhaibands. Lack of a sound foundation is like a boat tossing about at sea without a boatman to guide it to shore. What are their aims, their goals in life? The so-called wise men of the community have not bothered to reflect that the community would fall so low that it would be difficult to pull them out from the dark depths of the earth.

Our city's Amil community also has its inherent drawbacks. The difference between the Bhaibands and the Amils is that the Amils are aware of their faults and their elders guide the young people to rise above it all. The young, in turn, make an effort and hopefully they will succeed in bettering their lot. In contrast, our Sindhworki Bhaiband community has false pride. They are concerned only with counting their wealth and throwing it around but not for any constructive purpose.

No one has investigated whether this is right or wrong. No group, no society, no panchayat, no papers have brought to the forefront the pros and cons of these basic shortcomings. The Sindhworkis became a sect of their own and did not think it necessary to have the panchayat rule over them. They considered themselves above all, so the panchayat lost its hold on them and could not control them.

Comparison Between the Sethias of Yore and the Sethias of Today

The Bhaiband community still recalls the lifestyle of the Sethias of old. The most well-known Sethias of that time respected the community head, the mukhiya, and abided by the decisions of the panchayat. To be declared an outcaste by the panchayat was considered worse than death.

Because the Sethias respected the mukhiya, he in turn earned the respect of their partners and subordinates. The employer–employee relationship was a bond as strong as that of father and son. If a subordinate misbehaved, the Sethia's head would hang in shame. The Sethias knew that their behaviour, good or bad, would reflect not just on themselves, but on the entire community and city. As a result, they always set a good example. Their partners and employees followed suit and were always on their best behaviour. They consulted their Sethias not only on business matters, for which they were paid, but also on family matters. They knew they would get sound guidance.

Sethias of today consider it lowly to conform to the views of the panchayat. They think that because they have travelled the world over and seen upheavals in businesses, they are therefore more knowledgeable than these country bumpkins. Each Sethia strives to stand out, to have his name at the top of every list. He is so blinded by his wealth and subservience of his grovelling servants and sycophants that his vision is blurred. He thinks he has put Sindh on the map of the world. The Sindh that was hidden in one corner. So now he must rule here.

First and foremost, the Sindhworki Sethias detached themselves from the bonds of the panchayat in a very short time. While they succeeded in doing so, their partners and employees, who were always buzzing like bees around them, also sided with their Sethias. With the control of the panchayat gone, the Sethias could do what they liked and were answerable to none. They ruled the roost, made their own laws, and trampled those who tried to compete.

Secondly, they brainwashed the youth and inculcated drinking habits in them. Excise reports will disclose the amount of foreign liquor that came into Sindh. Leading the way were the Sindhworki Sethias, followed by their partners and lesser mortals of the Bhaiband community.

Thirdly, they introduced gambling. Their aim was to fragment the moveable and immoveable wealth so that no one should rise to the level of the Sethia in business and wealth. During the festival of Thadri (when snakes are worshipped) in the months of August and September, gambling went on through the night and losses and gains amounted to Rs 40,000–50,000. Many Sethias were so adept at gambling that they seldom lost and it became a way of life.

In this way the whole community was dumped in a death pit. The innocent partners did not realize this ploy, which was to always keep them at the Sethias' feet. And because the panchayat had no control, no one could pull out these poor devils, who then realized that they had been taken for a ride, but it was too late. One Sethia was even shameless enough to say, 'Other Sethias cheat in accounting, I beat them at cards!'

Dear brothers, you can well realize the downward slide of the community. If one is holding hands, everyone will come crashing down on each other.

 Soul-Searching

One can realize the state of conscience of these people. They are aware that virtues and vices exist in this world. However, according to them, these are not vices, it is merely entertainment and they firmly believe so. The Sethias are not alone in such thinking. Their partners and employees are not far behind. If they did not truly believe this, their conscience would have woken them up to the fact that this is pure cheating.

Many times the partners side with the Sethias and do not hesitate to ruin their own colleagues. When they are, in turn, mistreated by the Sethias, then they cry loud and clear, 'We sided with you against our friends and what did you give us? Ruination?!' I assure you, had the Sethias not pulled the wool over the eyes of their partners and encouraged them to indulge in vice, the partners would not have sided with the Sethias, and the Sethias would not have the strength to oppose the community.

Shri Krishna rightly told Duryodhan in the *Mahabharata*, 'Your wealth and strength has been founded on sinful ways. The food that you eat, the water that you drink, will obstruct sound thinking, and all those you touch will become like you. Even great men like Bhishma Pitamah and Dronacharya have lost the ability to speak the truth, and that is why you have their respect. But mine, you shall never have, because I represent Truth!'

These words are also applicable to the Sindhworki. They have amassed their wealth by fraudulent means. This has lessened their moral strength and instead of being truthful, they do not hesitate to speak lies and trample others underfoot.

38 Family Life of Sindhworkis

One may start out thinking that the Sindhworkis are not true to their country. They lack patriotism, they care not for the community, but surely they must love their families!

Alas, the Sindhworki cares only for himself. I tremble with rage when I see them pushing to the edge their loving, sincere wives and innocent children. They place their gentle babies on their laps and make them drink poisonous alcohol, taking delight in the way the babies reject or accept the drink. The same five- or six-year-olds then throw tantrums if they do not get a drink before meals.

They forcibly arrange parties for their wives where they make them drink till they are inebriated. Is this the magnanimity of the Sethias? Our daughters are taught to be good wives—to set up good homes and please their husbands. But when the husbands themselves find pleasure in such behaviour, what are the wives to do? These women were taught to walk on the path of truth and be strong in faith. Now our daughters-in-law will not even know how to roast a papad.

Today, our wives expect the following for a happy family life: a servant each for cooking, sweeping, swabbing and looking after the children. A carriage and a coachman for pleasure outings. Any amount of liquor. No interference of any kind. This is advancement. Households that do not conform to this pattern, strive to reach the standard before their sons and daughters come of age. No marriages take place in households that offer less than this. Our wives require that they should welcome their friends with an alcoholic drink. As a matter of fact, if the friends are not offered a hard drink, they consider it an insult. Few are those who decline to drink or would not eat a meal unless there is meat at the table—such decent girls are now treated as social outcasts.

One story goes that a daughter-in-law did not eat or drink at her in-laws' home for three days. The in-laws were delighted. But the reason was that she did not get alcohol with each meal, nor did she get non-vegetarian food. After three days, she returned to her parents' home. The in-laws thought they had an ideal daughter-in-law, and didn't realize she was used to alcohol and couldn't live without it, so she left the house.

The Sindhworki Sethias have set their own rules and believe them to be the foundation of a happy family and modern living. To this day, they strive for that modernization and feel they will touch the shore of happiness very soon.

39 Religious Zeal in Sindhworkis

The philanthropy of Hyderabadis is well known throughout the world. Every year, many *sadhus*, saints, y*ogis*, *sanyasis*, *brahmins* and *pindas* flock to Hyderabad. Some come for marriages of the children, some to grant boons for offspring, some to the opening of a new temple, some to perform *bhoomi puja* or to bless the digging of a well. The list is endless. Each one of them returns home with bulging haversacks.

East Hyderabad is worth visiting. To commemorate their success, or to keep alive the firm or family name, many Sethias have built small inns. Most of these are subsidized by Sindhworki Sethias. Some Bhaibands have added to this to make a show of the community. Numerous *Shivalayas* now dot the city. Whether these have actually increased religious fervour among the city dwellers or resulted in their attaining Heaven remains to be seen.

Those who built them have not once set foot in them. Some Sindhworkis have visited for *darshan* or worship. One can see that Sindhworkis were once a religious lot but because they lacked education, they were easily misled from the path of righteousness. Had there been some enthusiast who could have led them on the right path, they might have become better human beings, and the community and the country could have prospered beyond imagination.

40 Sindhwork Merchants Association

Anyone interested in understanding the mindset of the Sindhworki can do so by looking into the workings of the Sindhwork Merchants Association. There is a book on the subject, which is well worth reading. At first glance, one might like to praise those who established this organization in the service of the community. But upon closer inspection, it becomes evident that it's all an eyewash. The rules and regulations are all in favour of the Sethias, and not a thing has been done for the gains of the community or country.

Partners and employees alike felt that their last bit of freedom had been curtailed. For example, the rules state that no firm can employ anyone who leaves his job without the firm's certificate. No advances would be given to partners or employees. If they receive advances, it would be a certain percentage of their pay. No partner or employee can be a member of the Association.

Nothing has been done to raise the standard of the partners and employees. Those who are victimized have no representation in the Association to plead their cases.

At first, a few meetings were conducted, all for the gains of the Sethias. Then they closed the books/files, covered their heads and slept a sleep of peace. For the first six months some meetings were conducted—some suggestions made and some action taken, but none for the good of the country.

Sometime later, the Sindhworkis had a problem with their

passports. They wrote an application to the Commissioner of Sindh. When he came to Hyderabad, they met him and he recommended the Association be given the authority to issue passports. The Association, which had shut down, suddenly woke up! Meeting after meeting followed. Again to satisfy their own satanic lust for power and money, they ruled that only a member's employees would be issued passports through the Association. Piles of applications were sent to the Association and their treasury filled up. Each member paid an entry fee of Rs 25 plus Rs 2 per month and Re 1 for each employee's passport.

The pheriewallahs, the roving salesmen, were the ones who suffered. They begged the Association for passports. They said, 'We are individuals who take goods on credit and sell them abroad. Many times we have to borrow money for our fares. What do we do?' The Sethias said that for all practical purposes they were Sethias in their own right since they were self-employed.

In times gone by the Sethias would not admit even their lakhpati partner into the Association. After all, a partner is below their status, no matter how much he is worth. Now, for the sake of Rs 28, they do not hesitate to admit as member a pheriewallah or even a lowly cook.

The annual reports of the Sindhwork Merchants Association revealed that in the year 1917–1918, membership was only 40, but in the year 1918–1919, it jumped to 150! And all because of the commissioner authorizing the Association to issue passports. Most of these new members were pheriewallahs. The accounts showed a net profit of Rs 3,700. Twenty-seven meetings were held and the minutes declared as if a great service had been done for the public. No mention was made of the request to the commissioner or his order. So far, 449 passports had been granted. Now we are giving you a verbatim report:

The rule of the Association is that no passport application shall be entertained unless the applicant has cleared all dues and disputes with his former employer. This rule has facilitated the resolution of 37 such cases. One of the cases involved a member of the standing committee. His case was also settled through the Association. Were it not for the Association's authority, the employers would have had to approach the courts. Hopefully, the employees (not partners) will benefit from the Association's efforts to encourage out-of-court settlements.

At face value, these rules and regulations of the Association seem like good work. But now we will investigate its pros and cons and present the real picture before the reader.

I know for a fact that up to this time no partner had settled his disputes through the Association and the 37 cases mentioned above were of servants/employees. It should be recollected that at no time has any employee had outstanding dues from the Sethias. It has always been the Sethia who has cheated the employee. I can say without a doubt that these 37 settlements were in favour of the Sethias. The Association was instrumental in making the employees pay the Sethias—otherwise, no passport!

It is clear that the gain is the Sethia's who would otherwise have filed a suit against his employee and spent money and time on litigation. Even in litigation, the Sethia would have won and the poor servant burdened with expenses. The only time a servant outsmarted the Sethia was when he took all his money in advance and announced that he was dissatisfied with the Sethia's treatment. The Sethia, in a fit of anger, sent him back home. The fare costs anything between Rs 1,000 and Rs 1,500. The employee returned home and immediately took on a job with another Sethia. The previous Sethia filed a suit, and got a decree in his favour, but the servant had simply vanished by then.

Ultimately, the former Sethia was tired and, despite the decree, withdrew the case.

Now, with the Association's rules, the servants cannot get away. No clearance certificate, no passport. No passport, no employment. So the favours are only for the Sethias, and the servants were treated like bonded slaves!

Can anyone believe that a servant could pick up the courage to tell his boss that he wants to be treated as a human being? He knows he will never be able to get another job unless he pays back his advance money, fares and overheads, which the Sethia will slyly slap on to his debit column. His children and other dependants will starve. The only option for him is to bow and grovel before the Sethia. To try not to demand, but to beg like a dog to receive his dues.

In the olden days, the dissatisfied servants would, at the end of the contract, sweet talk the Sethia into giving them bonuses and then go and negotiate with other Sethias, take an advance, sign an agreement, and off they went on another journey. The former Sethia came to know only after the train left the platform or the ship left the docks.

The Sindhwork Merchants Association became a tool for the Sethias, and the servants were at their mercy every single day that passed and for each meal that they ate. Some say that if the servants were victimized, at least the lot of the partners improved. But how so?

Many partners were desirous of demanding their rights. But without membership in the Association, they had no voice. Since they were not Sethias, they were not eligible for membership. Of course, it did not come as a surprise to the partners that the rules and regulations of the Association did not include them. They knew who had set the stage and took part in the drama. They were happy that at least the Sethias were off their backs. In the end, the Association's conscience would not allow it to rest. A meeting was called and a suggestion presented that senior partners be given a chance to become members. The ruling passed unanimously. But to this day not one partner has joined. They feel they will be treated as underdogs so they prefer to stay out. How right they were!

A meeting of the Association was called for recommendation for passports. I was present at that meeting. I would like the reader to know the facts.

At the said meeting, a servant approached the president of the Association for recommendations for issuance of a passport. The hall was packed and at least 50 to 60 Sethias were among the audience. As per routine, the servant was asked whether he had worked for any Sethia and if all his accounts were clear and all differences settled.

> **Servant:** I have not worked anywhere before this. I had settled with so and so Sethia but now he declines to take me. I have no outstanding with him.

The Sethia was then called upon to give his evidence.

> **President:** Have you any objections—physical, moral, or financial?
>
> **Sethia:** I object. His accounts with me are not clear and I think there may be some outstanding.

I remember the occasion. I looked at the man. He gave a start and went red in the face with fury. For some time he kept staring at the Sethia. Then he controlled himself and, with great humility, turned to the president and said, 'Sir, I don't owe anything to him. I am positive about it. One and a half years ago, I signed an agreement with the Sethia. Since then I have been going to him and urging him to send me on a journey. Today, after one and a half years of being jobless, he tells me he has no need for me. I paid money for the agreement and passport out of my own pocket.' The president then requested both the parties to meet him at home to come to a decision. In the meantime, the passport issue was shelved.

When the proceedings were over, one of the Sethias stood up and in a loud voice raised an objection before the whole assembly, condemning the behaviour of the servants in front of their Sethias. He said that they must be taught to be subservient before their masters. He was supported by the rest of the Sethias.

The next day, the servant presented himself before the president. There was no sight of the Sethia. The president put up a recommendation for the servant's passport considering him to be telling the truth and gave him the benefit of the doubt. Is it likely that the members raised an objection? The president himself was a Sethia, and there should have been a hue and cry over his decision—but no, not at all! The assembly must have thought that the Sethia felt insulted by just the look of the servant. How much more degrading is it that one of their colleagues should openly lie, just to bring the fellow to book? Not one member objected. Can you imagine how much value the Sethias have for truth? This is why the junior partners declined membership of the Association. As members, they would have to keep their mouths shut or be 'yes men' to the Sethia—either way was undesirable!

I apologize for straying away from the subject. I was caught up in a maze of cases. Now I come back to the Association's working.

When the Association decided to admit senior partners, one such person requested the members that he would like to join the Association if he was assured that his case would get a just hearing, or else he would not like to waste his entry membership fee of Rs 25. He said that his brother-in-trade died, leaving behind a destitute widow. For the last 6 to 8 months, he had been requesting the Sethia to give her husband's dues, but he refused to comply.

The president put the case before the standing committee.

The following decision was attained:

> According to our rules, both parties must voluntarily agree to our arbitration. If either refuses, we can do nothing. For servants, we act solely on the Sethia's word. For partners, both sides must agree.

Dear reader, you can well realize that the bosses themselves openly decline such decisions and have not an iota of consideration for the public. If in open assemblies they can behave as they like, how much more must they be terrorizing their subordinates in their homes, where there are no witnesses, and the rules and regulations are of their own making.

Note: The Association now recommends passport issuance even in the absence of employee clearance or no-objection certificates.

41. Penance

I do not consider myself eligible to advise such a wealthy, famous and courageous community but, with folded hands and on bended knees, I request the Sindhworkis to reflect on these happenings with a cool head and think of your duty towards your community and country. When the gaunt faces of those who have died due to your lack of caring or those who live like the dead because of your treatment dance before your eyes, you will cry out, 'What shall I do?' Your insatiable desire for wealth does not allow you to see your own downfall. Look within. Search your conscience, and I'm sure that one day you will realize the impending doom looming above you and it will shake you into realizing the truth. When you recognize the wrongs you have committed and the lives that have been ruined because of your greed, you will question yourself, 'What should I do?' Your conscience will stir. It will not allow you to rest. Do some soul-searching and act now!

Open your lockers and your hearts. Distribute the wealth you have collected through the blood of your servants among those who have nothing. There is no charity greater than the gift of education and knowledge. With your ill-gotten gains, educate the people and help your motherland.

You are well known for your donations to religious institutions, but help your country and Goddess Laxmi will bless you and your offspring and you will be remembered for generations to come.

This humble soul entreats all Sindhworkis, be they Sethias or partners, employees or servants, to buy a copy of this book.

Read and reflect upon the contents and strive to improve and implement a system so that it becomes a shining example for the whole world.

My brethren, I shall now conclude by seeking forgiveness for all that I have disclosed.

***Namaskar. Asro Guru Jo.* Goodbye.**

Acknowledgements

This book owes its existence to the dedication and contributions of several thoughtful individuals. Padmini Mirchandani, a family friend, has been both a creative and conceptual guide throughout the making of this book, which includes the translation of her grandfather's own work on the Sindhworkis. My cousin, Usha Bhandarkar, has been a companion and guide through the earliest drafts to the final version, offering her intimate knowledge of family episodes over the years.

I am grateful to Nandita Bhavnani, noted Sindh historian and author, and Sahib Bijani, Director of the Indian Institute of Sindhology in Adipur-Gandhidham, for their meticulous insights and corrections regarding language and context.

Arlene D'souza designed a cover that evocatively captures the spirit of the book and carried the vision through to the inner pages.

I thank my friend Shobhaa De who, through literary agent Kanishka Gupta, introduced me to Dibakar Ghosh at Rupa Publications, making the publication of this book possible. Thanks are also due to his team at Rupa, especially Shatarupa Dhar, whose gentle persistence and eye for detail helped shape the book into its present form.

—Manjeet Kripalani

Glossary

Aarti	A Hindu ritual of worship, in which light from a flame is offered to deities
Andaaz	Approximation; a rough estimate or intuitive measurement, especially in cooking
Anna	A former Indian coin worth one-sixteenth of a rupee; obsolete after decimalization in 1957
Ashram	A spiritual hermitage or monastery; a retreat for religious learning and meditation
Asro Guru Jo	A Sindhi phrase meaning 'May the blessings of the Guru be with you', often used as a respectful farewell or benediction
Atta	Whole wheat flour used primarily for making Indian breads
Attar	Natural perfume oil derived from botanical sources such as flowers and herbs
Badaam–pistajo varo	A thin, brittle sweet made of finely sliced almonds and pistachios, often garnished with poppy seeds
Baksheesh	A tip, bribe or charitable donation, commonly given in South Asian cultures
Basmati rice	A fragrant, long-grain rice variety traditionally grown in the Indian subcontinent, prized for its aroma and texture
Baug	Garden; often used to refer to well-maintained ornamental or public gardens
Besan kadhi	A traditional North Indian dish made of gram flour (besan) and yoghurt, spiced and often served with rice

Bhajan-kirtan	Devotional singing, often in praise of Hindu deities, performed in religious gatherings
Bhajjia	Deep-fried savoury fritters made with vegetables and gram flour batter; also known as pakoras
Bharela bhindi	Stuffed okra; a spiced vegetable dish made with okra filled with seasoned stuffing
Bhoomi puja	A Hindu ritual performed before the construction of a building, to honour and seek permission from the Earth goddess and to ensure the project proceeds without obstacles
Bhoot khana	Haunted house; a place believed to be inhabited by spirits
Bochhan	Scarves, often embroidered or gifted as part of trousseaux
Bori chops	A meat dish made with mutton chops, typically prepared in Sindhi cuisine
Burqa	A veil or outer garment worn by some Muslim women, symbolizing modesty and religious observance
Chana dal	Split Bengal gram; a type of lentil commonly used in Indian cooking
Charpoys	Traditional woven bedsteads or cots made with a wooden frame and interlaced rope or jute
Chowmasa	A traditional fasting period of four months in the Hindu calendar, observed during the monsoon season (from Ashadh to Kartik), marked by abstinence from non-vegetarian food and certain rituals
Dada	A respectful term for an elder or grandfather in Sindhi culture

Dambar lagaalo	A colloquial phrase in Hindi/Sindhi, literally meaning 'put tar on it', often used metaphorically to imply 'cover it up' or 'ignore it'
Darbar	A royal court or formal assembly held by a ruler; also refers to the hall where such meetings take place
Darshan	A devotional act of seeing or being seen by a deity or a holy person
Dulhan	The bride; a woman on her wedding day or newly married
Durry	A handwoven rug or thin flat carpet, typically made from cotton
Faujdar	A historical title used during the British Raj/Mughal times, referring to a military commander or law enforcer in charge of a district or region
Gaddi	A seat or throne; symbolically represents authority or succession
Ghungroos	Ankle bells worn by classical Indian dancers, especially during performances
Gopis	The cowherd maidens devoted to Lord Krishna, often symbolizing divine love
Guru dakshina	A traditional offering or token of gratitude to one's teacher
Haaris	Agricultural labourers or tenants who work on a landlord's land, especially in Sindh
Hooris	Beautiful, celestial maidens described in Islamic tradition as companions in paradise
Kakhpatis	Paupers; those who possess little or no wealth (in contrast to lakhpatis)

Karela stuffed with kheema	Bitter gourd stuffed with spiced minced meat
Kavelu	Clay roof tiles traditionally used in rural houses across India; also used metaphorically to indicate a humble home
Khansamas	Cooks or chefs, especially those in royal or colonial kitchens in India
Khes	A handwoven cotton throw, used as a cover during sleep in the harsh summer months
Kidney-liver bheja	A rich preparation made with offal, including kidneys, liver and brain
Kohira/Kabuli chana	Chickpeas; a staple legume used in various Indian dishes
Lakhpatis	Millionaires; individuals who possess wealth amounting to lakhs (hundreds of thousands)
Loli	A type of Sindhi flatbread often prepared with or without spices
Lungi-poti	Bonuses promised to an employee at the end of his contract
Maang-tikka	A traditional ornament worn by women in Indian culture, on the forehead near the parting line of the hair
Maiya	Mother; a colloquial or affectionate term
Masi	Aunty; refers to one's mother's sister
Mawa	Milk solids obtained by reducing milk; used in Indian sweets
Meenakari	A traditional art of decorating metal surfaces with enamel painting, especially in jewellery
Meetha lolo	A traditional sweet Sindhi flatbread made with wheat flour, jaggery, ghee, and cardamom

Mehendi	Henna; a dye used to create decorative patterns, especially on hands and feet
Methiji macchi	Fish cooked with fenugreek leaves
Mir	A title of nobility or military general
Mirzadi	The wife of a Mir
Moong dal	Split yellow mung beans; used extensively in Indian cooking for dals (lentil stews) and savoury snacks
Mujras	Dance performances by courtesans or nautch girls, often seen in royal or aristocratic courts
Mukhiya/ Chaudhary/ Pancha	The headman or chief of a village or community
Mukhtiarkar	A local revenue officer or collector in the administrative system
Mungh	A unique architectural feature that acted as a natural air-conditioning system
Mureeds	Disciples or followers, especially in a Sufi religious context
Murmala	Fried strands of gram flour, often eaten as a crunchy snack
Muth	A monastic community; a religious institution or sect
Nagar	A town or small city
Nariyal-ji-mithai	Sweets made from grated coconut and condensed milk
Navaar	A strong cotton tape used in traditional Indian charpoys (woven beds) for support
Neem	Indian lilac tree known for its medicinal properties

Paaee	A small unit of currency, where 3 paaees equal to 1 paisa, used in pre-independence India and Sindh
Paapar–pani	Crisp lentil wafers (papads) served with flavoured water or as snacks
Pahakaa	Traditional sayings expressing commonly held wisdom or truths, often passed down through generations
Paisa	A subunit of the Indian rupee; 100 paise equal 1 rupee. Historically, 64 paise made a rupee before decimalization
Panchayat	A traditional village council or governing community body
Panzeb	Anklet; ornamental jewellery worn around the ankle
Pawas	Supports or legs; often refers to the legs of a cot or table
Pingha	A traditional hanging seat used in Sindhi homes, often suspended from the ceiling by ropes or chains. The pingha was used by both children and adults for rest, play, or leisure, and was commonly found in courtyards or verandas
Pir	A Muslim spiritual guide or holy man, particularly in Sufism
Pistan-ji-mithai	Pistachio-based sweets, typical of Sindhi confectionery
Prasad	A devotional offering made to a deity, later distributed to devotees
Pugree	A turban; also refers to a token amount paid in tenancy to secure property rights (in some legal contexts)

Glossary • 301

Purdah	The religious and social practice of female seclusion from public observation
Raas	A traditional folk dance and drama, especially associated with Krishna and the Gopis
Raja	A king or prince; a ruler of a region
Runk	A pauper; someone of low or no financial means
Samosa	A deep-fried savoury pastry with a filling of spiced potatoes, peas, or meat
Sant/Sadhu/Yogi/Sanyasi/Brahmin/Pinda	Terms denoting various kinds of religious ascetics, holy men and spiritual practitioners in Hinduism
Satsang	A spiritual discourse or gathering in the company of truth and devotion
Sherbet	A sweetened drink made with diluted fruit juice or flavoured syrup
Shivalayas	Temples or shrines dedicated to Lord Shiva
Shravan	A sacred month in the Hindu lunar calendar (July–August), associated with devotion to Lord Shiva and marked by fasting and religious observances
Streedhan	Gifts, property or wealth given to a woman by her family at the time of her wedding
Taluka	An administrative district or sub-division, akin to a county
Tava	A flat griddle used for baking or roasting bread such as chapatis or parathas
Thadri festival	A traditional Sindhi festival dedicated to Goddess Shitala, celebrated with fasting and eating cold food prepared the previous day to honour the goddess of cooling and health

Tikki	A spiced potato cutlet or patty, often shallow-fried and eaten as a snack
Titar	Partridge; a game bird often featured in traditional cuisine
Toori	A type of gourd; also known as ridge gourd or sponge gourd
Vishal	Magnificent; grand or vast in scale
Wah-wah	An exclamation of admiration or praise
Zamindars/ Thakurs	Landowners

www.ingramcontent.com/pod-product-compliance
Lightning Source LLC
Chambersburg PA
CBHW020831160426
43192CB00007B/609